Memoirs
of a
C Student

Don White CDs

Live in Michigan (2003)

It's a Great Day (DVD) (2002)

Little Niche (2001)

Brown Eyes Shine (1999)

Rascal (1996)

Live at the Somerville Theatre (1995)

Two Vagabonds in Disguise (1992)

www.DonWhite.net

Memoirs
of a
C Student

by

Don White

Barry Park Press
Lynn, Massachusetts

First printing October 2006
Second printing October 2007
Third printing September 2010
Fourth printing October 2015

Cover art and design by Mark McInerney

For booking information:

booking@DonWhite.net
617-539-3182
www.DonWhite.net

ISBN 0-9789741-1-5

Printed in the United States of America
by King Printing, Inc., Lowell, Massachusetts

This book is dedicated to my mother and father,
Larry and Frannie White, who built a life for my brother,
my sister, and me that they could only have dreamed
about for themselves when they were young.

Contents

Foreword

I am not supposed to be a writer. I have always suspected that prior to my birth I inadvertently stepped in front of a writing arrow that was aimed at the ass of some rich kid.

I'm sure that somewhere there is a man my age, born to great wealth, who dropped out of school, picked up an addiction or two, pissed away a fortune, screwed up a marriage and wound up banging nails for a living, who suspects that someone else is living out his destiny.

It's like that cartoon where the drunken stork delivers the kangaroo baby to the mouse family.

People like me are supposed to be drawn to the inner workings of the combustion engine so we can learn a trade and support ourselves. It puts us at a tremendous economic disadvantage when we are drawn instead to the inner workings of something as impractical as the soul.

I know that writers are born to all segments of society but it is not fair. The compulsion to write is a curse for a working class person because it mandates a life of distraction. A schoolboy infected at birth with the writer's disease cannot possibly excel in his metal shop class because he is genetically compelled to spend his school day looking out of the window and imagining a random series of ridiculous scenarios. (That's why it's important that shop teachers quickly identify writers (and stoners) and keep their precious extremities away from power tools.)

A writer's propensity for daydreaming can best be developed into a marketable skill if he is born to wealth and can fill the years of his youth with travel, contemplation, philosophy, and literature.

So, destiny's poor marksmanship delivered unto me the most useless of all talents for survival in a blue-collar world —a mind of persistent impractical creative distraction.

And thus I have lived the life of the cab driver poet— working long hours for small pay while secretly utilizing my drive time, coffee breaks, and weekends to feed my writing compulsion.

I have always loved prose. When I was twelve years old I had an electric typewriter in my room upon which I composed bad fiction. I continued to do so until my early twenties when my wife and I started our family. One big problem that a young parent will encounter with the writing of prose is that it requires the most elusive of all things to a mom or dad: quiet time. In early adulthood, due primarily to the scarcity of the aforementioned quiet time, I abandoned prose and devoted my creative energy exclusively to songwriting. The fact that I could call up the melody of a half-written song at any free moment and that the lyric-in-progress would be attached to that melody in my mind made it possible to write songs while driving to and from work.

By May of 2001 my music career had finally arrived at a place where I could justify the decision to go part-time at my day job. I suddenly found myself with two mornings a week where the house was empty and quiet.

I decided to write a book. How hard could that be, I thought? I'd just whip it out in a couple of months and then move on to something else.

Today is May 20th, 2006. I have devoted all of my irreplaceable free time for five years to this ill-advised endeavor, to the complete exclusion of the songwriting that has helped to sustain my family for a decade and a half. I have no publisher. I don't have enough money to print the books myself. And I have found precious few examples of songwriters who have turned a profit on prose. It's as if as a folksinger I was determined to find the one other enterprise on earth that would demand significantly more time and creative energy with the potential to generate less money.

In the next few days I need to think of a title for this collection of short stories. Here are two ideas that I am considering.

Boondoggle: The Unmarketable Memoirs of a C Student
and
Tailspin: How Writing This Book Killed my Tiny Folk Career

Economic inviability notwithstanding, I have, on a creative level, benefited tremendously from my five-year marriage to this project. The freedom from rhyme, meter, and all the other constraints of songwriting has been exhilarating. Over time I had come to see songs as stories confined to little boxes. Songwriting is fraught with rules and limitations. And try as I might to punch out the walls of the little story containers I, like every other writer of songs, am ceilinged, if you will, by the restrictions inherent in the medium.

Songs need to rhyme.

Songs can't be too long.

Songs have to be at least somewhat musical.

You are permitted, I suppose, to meander a bit with the music, but a meandering lyric in a song that intends to tell a story is a recipe for a forgettable song.

"Don't bore us. Get to the chorus."

Upon my escape from songwriting prison in 2001 I sat before my computer to tell a tale. When I looked up four hours had passed and the story I had intended to tell was nowhere to be found. Instead there was a much more interesting adventure on the screen before me that had found its way to the surface of my mind via the mysterious creative freedom inherent in the writing of prose. It was intoxicating. I was intoxicated. I floated down the stairs to the living room where I sat on the couch in a semi-dream state with a curious grin on my face until the spell was broken by my wife when she came home from work and asked me what I had been doing all day.

In order to fully grasp the magnitude of my subsequent hopeless addiction to this process one would need to take into consideration my lifelong compulsion to write and my addictive personality. One would also, I suspect, need to know something about what the hell goes on inside the head of a writer. Don't even bother. It's like a fever dream in there —frenzied imagination. I'm sure that today's young writers are being prescribed something to tone down, or eliminate altogether, this unrestrained freethinking.

As imagination continues its inevitable march toward the endangered species list, let me at least try to communicate to you the degree to which my unmedicated imagination has enriched my life.

*****

As a lover of language I hate to acknowledge its weaknesses. However, I do understand that there are circumstances that shine a very bright light on the ineptitude of language as a means of communication. For an excellent example of the inability of language to accurately express, for instance, deep emotion, one need look no further than the funeral of a friend. What words could possibly come out of your mouth that would do justice to the profound heartache you feel for the sister of your friend at the loss of her brother? Even a normally innocuous question like "how are you?" is an obscenely ridiculous thing to say in this situation. "How am I? Well, let's see. I'm standing next to my dead brother and his weeping children, my heart is ripped to shreds, and for three days I've felt as if I'd just been punched in the stomach. I'm gonna have to go with . . . not so good."

In this situation, eye contact, a touch on the shoulder or a hug is infinitely more articulate than any words a person could utter. Similarly, the look in a man's eye as he tries to describe his moment of spiritual awakening is always much more eloquent than the particular assemblage of sounds he chooses to use.

This is why poets always seem otherworldly to me. A good poet will approach these big ideas knowing that the tools with which he intends to build his word palace are primitive at best. Building the Taj Mahal with the equivalent of a rock and a stick is the daily miracle of the journeyman poet.

Not being a poet, I anticipate that the word palace at the end of this description will be more back yard tree house than Taj Mahal.

Let's take a look at one of the more challenging of the big ideas upon which a poet might attempt to build a word castle. I'm talking, of course, about love. Love is in that prestigious category of concepts like freedom, creativity, and God that constantly mock language and dare it to describe them. Each of these concepts seems to have no limits upon how deeply it can be understood. Each also has the remarkable ability to make you feel that you have a complete understanding of them no matter where you are in your own personal development when they are encountered.

Let's assume that when you fell in love for the first time you were a teenager and you didn't know shit about love. But at the instant your lips touched the lips of your first sweetheart you became a virtual encyclopedia on the subject. Your experience with love was so complete and consuming at that moment in your life that the idea that there could be more to it was incomprehensible.

Several years later you were looking into the eyes of your first-born child. The love you felt for that baby bore no resemblance to the love you felt when you were in your teens. It seemed almost criminal to use the same word for both experiences. There is nothing linking your teenage love and the love you felt for your firstborn except for the inescapable fact that they each felt complete and consuming at the time you were experiencing them.

Now you're ninety. You've outlived all your siblings, your spouse, and two of your children. It's Thanksgiving. There is no reason to believe that it will not be your last. The child of your child has brought your first great-granddaughter to your home and placed her upon your knee. The infant is looking up at you and smiling as you sing her a nursery rhyme that your grandmother taught you eighty-five years ago.

Can anyone under the age of ninety, witnessing this scene, possibly comprehend, let alone attempt to describe, the depth of the love that you feel in your heart at this moment?

Every loss you have suffered, every accomplishment you have made, and every single waking moment of your life have all conspired to continually deepen your understanding of love while simultaneously making you feel that each individual expanded moment of comprehension was full and complete. At no point along the way did you suspect that there might be deeper levels of love than the one you were experiencing.

Although there is a lesser degree of emotional intensity, freedom behaves much the same way as love in our hearts and minds. The experience of freedom in the mind of the two-year-old who escapes his playpen and runs laughing through the living room is as complete as that of the retiree who sells off his possessions, moves to a cabin in the country, and fills his remaining days with the activities of his choosing.

One of the stories in this collection is called "The Boys Club." In it, I reflect upon the tremendous amount of personal freedom I had as a child and how it has shaped my view of the world. When I was seventeen I embarked upon a three-year hitchhiking adventure. By my early twenties my understanding of the word "freedom" had been significantly expanded by my childhood and by those three years of having nothing to go back to, no one to answer to, and nothing to get out of my sleeping bag for.

Freedom is a very big word to me.

Upon my return to the workforce from freedom's highway

I quickly discovered that an independent streak and a visceral contempt for authority were conspicuously absent from the list of desirable job applicant qualifications. The unique set of skills that I brought to my first few job interviews via the hitchhiking life seemed to be much less impressive to my prospective employers than, for example, obedience. However, since I was now in the baby-making business I was forced to lasso my independent streak and keep it tied and gagged in my basement.

One night, when time and energy finally permitted, and after everyone was asleep, I tiptoed to the basement and unleashed my independent spirit. He responded like a hyperactive puppy that had been caged all day—running in circles, bouncing straight up and down, and pleading with a mouth of froth for me to let him run wild. It broke my heart to tell him that my world had persona non grata'd him—that he had become, in effect, a financial liability to me. He seemed completely inconsolable and borderline suicidal until I revealed to him that his services were still in great demand within the narrow confines of my songwriting.

Relinquishing my personal freedom in the "earning a living" part of my life only caused me to defend it more tenaciously in my creative life. With the invaluable support of my inexhaustible independent streak, I have bent, broken, stepped around, ignored, and taken unforgivable liberties with every rule I have encountered in songwriting.

At one point in my life I was so fed up with being told that songs needed a bridge and a chorus that I decided to write a song that had only one note in it. This turned out to be a little too ambitious. The final result was a song called "The MTV Love Song" that has no chorus, no bridge, very simple chords, and three verses with three different emotional agendas. It is among the most unmarketable songs ever penned. I couldn't care less. I am not addicted to financial success. I am addicted to creative freedom and, in all honesty, to being a brat.

I am quite proud of the fact that I was able to find a way to keep my independent streak from withering away altogether. But over time it became obvious that only allowing him to run within the confines of my songwriting was a lot like just moving him into a bigger cage.

Some years later he told me that when I was finally able to turn him loose on prose it was the first time in twenty years that he was able to experience a sense of freedom that rivaled our hitchhiking years.

While we were writing that first story he kept turning around to me and saying, "This doesn't have to rhyme, right? I can take as long as I want and use as many words as I feel are appropriate to express this thought, right? If I get an idea that is interesting, but only peripheral to the main story I have the freedom to branch off and explore it, right?" And each time I would nod in agreement beaming with pride that I was finally able to let him run in a field without fences.

Now we have come to the part of this foreword where language seems completely ill-equipped for the job at hand.

Come on, kids. Let's build a tree house.

I was once told this by a friend of mine who is a great artist: "You know what you are doing is art if it removes you from the constraints of time." I think this hypothesis is a bit of an oversimplification with more than a few holes in it. For example, I have had sexual intercourse that has removed me from the constraints of time (three and a half minutes still counts as time, right?) but I find it very unlikely that the other participant in this performance would describe it as a masterpiece.

That being said, I do love the concept.

In the process of writing this book I have on several occasions been completely removed from any connection to time whatsoever. Honestly, I would emerge from a passage and have absolutely no idea if I had been writing for ten minutes or three hours. I had had some experience with this as a songwriter so, although pleasantly intoxicating, it was not unprecedented.

However, this other thing began to happen that was so creatively orgasmic that if the acquiring of it required money I would, from the instant of my first exposure, have had a five-hundred-dollar-a-day habit.

I would sit before my computer and begin to write with a very specific tale to tell. A few minutes into the telling of that tale a disheveled raconteur with a different story in mind would begin to tap at my window. I had heard this tapping all my life but the constraints of songwriting combined with the limited free time that my life allotted for creative endeavors always forced me to shoo him away as if he were a stray dog or a flock of pigeons.

One day I opened the window and the half-crazy vagabond with a pocket full of stories who had been loitering on the stairwells of my creative life for forty years climbed in and sat beside me. I trusted him implicitly. I thanked him for his patience. I then relinquished any attachment to my original intent and let him talk.

And for the first time in my life I let my stories tell themselves to me.

Language fails me here. I seem to have only clichés in my vocabulary. And this world simply cannot spare any more oxygen for another self-absorbed writer referring to himself as a conduit for the muse.

I cannot speak to the why or the how of the creative process. But I instinctively reject the idea that Mother Muse is stocking the lake with brilliant songs and stories and that some writers are just better fishermen than others. I reject this idea because it removes power from me. I hate fishing because the fish is in control.

I can only speak from experience.

I have observed the songwriting process in the hands of some brilliant songsmiths. It is mystifying to me. First an interesting guitar lick appears of its own volition and then slowly leads the writer to a partial lyric. The writer nurtures these musical and lyrical seedlings until eventually they flower into something resembling a song and then, at the time of their choosing, the music and lyric reveal to the writer the song's content.

My songwriting process holds no mystery whatsoever. It is a magic-free zone. Here, I can explain it to you in a couple of sentences.

I experience something in my life. I deal with it. When it is over and I have had some time to process the entire experience I look back on it and write a song about it using humor, heart, or both as a template. That's it.

I do not like to participate in songwriting workshops because my process is completely demystified and seems a bit unworthy. I have always felt more like a song carpenter than a song writer.

So imagine my surprise when during the writing of this book I discovered that I could begin the process and antici-pate with relative certainty that something much more interesting than my prefabricated story idea would slip into my pen and drag me and my cumbersome preconceptions by the hand to a new adventure.

I am the classic addictive personality. I have tethered myself to several substances and behaviors in my life, secretly hoping that one of them would fulfill my lust for adventure. What a glorious moment it was for me to stumble upon an activity that promised the unforeseen. To describe what it meant to me at the age of forty-four to discover a process so intoxicating that it labeled every mind-altering substance a cheap imitation and promised to inject wonder into all my remaining days is completely beyond my ability.

This kind of writing is a daydreamer's dream job. Is it possible that I could actually get paid for letting my imagination have its way with me?

Well, getting paid is a matter of some conjecture at this point—no matter. If I had undertaken this project expecting to retire comfortably from the profits, I would have to give serious consideration to *Don White's Folly* as a title.

I am standing at the threshold of my sixth decade. Not surprisingly, my understanding of what it means to drink deeply of life today, at age forty-nine, bears no resemblance whatsoever to the many varied perspectives I have had on this subject in decades past.

Today is Sunday. I have to work at my day job tomorrow. I have given another weekend to this book—not just any weekend, but one of those glorious midsummer New England weekends so rare that they can be counted annually on one hand. I watched this entire weekend come and go peripherally outside my window as if it were a program on a muted television.

This life I have created has shown very little interest in giving serious consideration to any of the proposals I have brought before its board of directors regarding the possibility of moving the corporation in a direction that might generate the kind of revenue that would, in turn, make available to me the abundance of free time that is routinely granted to writers of privilege.

I have come to believe that it is in the board's interest to keep me sprinting from one job to another in order to pay my mortgage and keep my family fed because they quite rightly assume that if I were ever granted a significant block of free time I would use it to question their authority and their relevance.

So, if my life continues to force me to choose between using my precious free time living or being cooped up somewhere writing about the living I have already done, I will choose to have the sun on my face. I will choose to have tea with someone I love. I will even choose to do the unthinkable: walk without earphones and take in the sounds of my world.

Writing this book has been the most difficult creative undertaking of my life. I have never participated in anything so time-consuming, burdensome, and frustrating. There were times when I felt buried alive beneath the fucking thing. Unless, by some miracle, this book generates enough money to hurl me into a life where free time is not a rare and endangered bird, I will never do this again.

Writing this book has been the most exhilarating creative experience of my life. Through the process I have touched the face of my formative years. I have seen, laid out before me, an extraordinary creative pathway that I expect to walk upon for the rest of my days. I owe my newfound creative freedom to this experience. But unless, by some miracle, this book generates enough money to hurl me into a life where free time is not a rare and endangered bird, I will never do this again.

I have given five years of my free time to this beast. It has promised me nothing in return except that it will not give me back any of the days I surrendered to it.

July 16th, 2006

Abandon hope all ye who enter here.

(If you *hope* to find any truth within these pages, that is.)

At the risk of front-loading this book so severely that the reader dies of boredom before reaching the first story, I feel that it is important that I include this disclaimer.

Let me say this plainly. This book is a pack of lies. The lying begins with the use of the word "memoirs" in the title and proliferates exponentially from there.

Memoirs? Get real. I'm almost fifty years old. I can't remember where I parked my car.

Most of these stories take place between 1962 and 1992. There are a few things in here that I think I remember but it is just as likely that I dreamed them. Any events described herein that I believed to be true have been so modified via my bad memory and the liberties I have allowed myself in describing them that they now qualify only as fiction.

I therefore have decided to change the names of all but a few of the characters.

During the renaming process I discovered that there is no science to the creating of fake names for real people, because the names I made up off the top of my head seem just as believable as the ones I created by transposing the first and last names of musicians from Frank Zappa's bands.

Memoirs
of a
C Student

A Woman Between Worlds

Part One
That Funny Folksinger

One

How many folksingers does it take to screw in a light bulb?

Two.

One to screw in the new bulb and one to write a song about the dead one.

Folk is the crazy aunt of the music business—annoying and uncooperative but still part of the family. Through the years there have been many discussions on the subject of having her institutionalized. But for now the family seems content to keep her locked away in the attic.

I am a folksinger. I embrace the term. I do not partake in the creation of diversionary new names for what I do. I suppose that I could call myself a singer-songwriter or an alternative or acoustic performing artist. But the road to euphemism is paved with insecurity. Singing, songwriting, alternative, acoustic, performing artists can, at times, be a bit insecure about calling themselves folksingers because they know that most Americans hate folk music. One of the most easily defended reasons for hating folk music is that it's boring. Boring is bad enough all by itself but when you add a dash of preachy, a cup of navel gazing, and an ounce of unsweetened self-righteousness, you have what, for a significant percentage of the population, is a recipe for a very unpopular pot of excruciating stew.

But I love it—not because it is boring, I endure that. I love it because I love being in the company of people who choose the path of impoverished integrity over fame at any cost. I derive great comfort from being part of a community that nurtures the development of its young and fragile members and encourages them to find their own voice, knowing full well that, in all likelihood, a day job will be required to subsidize that voice.

While all of her supposedly sane relatives will happily mold you into a replica of whatever is trendy, it is only your crazy aunt that will support your desire to do something of substance.

The relationship I have with folk music I also have with comedy. The handful of people who excel in either field impact my life so significantly that I would gladly walk barefoot across a mile of smoldering lyrical mediocrity to get to one John Prine. I would likewise gleefully endure the predictable slings and arrows of one thousand angry, dysfunctional, racist, lowest-common-denominator, dick-joke-telling, entirely derivative, entirely forgettable white standup comedians to see two minutes of work by Richard Pryor.

It's like panning for gold. Whatever it takes to get to the big nugget is fine.

Before I began going to open mikes and trying to build my acoustic, solo, alternative, singer-songwriter, humorist career, I only performed twice a year. Every spring and fall from 1982 to 1990 I would rent the function hall at the American Legion in Lynn, Massachusetts and produce something called the Don White and Friends Show. I would assemble a band of local musicians. We would have a few rehearsals and then bang out a show. The audience consisted primarily of friends, family and work associates—proletarians one and all. Serving up a bowl of excruciating folk stew to these people who only considered Saturday night a success if they had no recollection of it on Sunday was not an option. They wanted to go wild. We encouraged them.

Sometimes the crowd at these shows was so small that there wasn't enough money from the door to pay the band. But most of the shows were packed. The well-attended nights always featured that palpable sense of impending danger that comes to life whenever you combine unlimited drugs and alcohol with loud music and crazy people. The audiences at the Don and Friends Shows were, as you might expect, not exactly predisposed to musical or lyrical nuance. Mr. Subtlety was persona non grata. Everything had to be over the top.

The first half of the show consisted of several skits where, during certain songs, the band would change costumes, recite dialogue in character, and act out different comedy routines. The second half was a rock and roll dance party.

For several years our concerts held the Legion Hall single event record for alcohol consumption—no small accomplishment in a factory town.

In the eighties a noteworthy percentage of the audience (and the occasional band member) were completely amped out on cocaine. After the show, guys I worked with would come up to me with their eyes rolling around in their heads. They would be grinding their teeth and doing weird things with their lips as they tried to express how their lives had been changed by the show. "Man, this is the greatest band ever! You guys should be on television! I'm going home right now and I'm going to call the Tonight Show. No. Really. I mean it. They've gotta have you guys on there."

Unfortunately, the recordings of these performances did not always justify the enthusiasm of the blow monkeys in the audience.

I learned many things from my experiences with the Don and Friends Shows. One of the more interesting pieces of knowledge I acquired was this: it is possible that the band that generates the most excitement is the band with the most tweaked-out audience. This is called GDS (Grateful Dead Syndrome).

I really loved doing those shows. I loved the idea of the band members being active participants in the theatrical nature of the performance. Thinking up new skits and trying them out on stage was always very exciting for me. I brought this concept of a concert that was more than music with me later when I found my way into the performing songwriter world.

Two

I quit drinking for a few months in 1987. The subsequent insomnia and my unwillingness to sit in a bar without imbibing created a gigantic windfall of time in my life. I very quickly went from not having enough time to finish anything that I had started to being buried alive beneath an avalanche of free time.

It turns out that the party life is a full-time job—a couple of hours every weekday after work at the local bar, all night Friday, all night Saturday and a little maintenance on Sunday—that's gotta be in the vicinity of forty hours. Christ, if you look at it in terms of unproductive time—if you factor the hangovers into the equation, it's like having two full-time jobs.

I started going to open mikes in Boston and Cambridge. I was very fortunate because I began to pick up gigs right away. (I called them gigs but they were just opportunities to play for free for half an hour to small audiences that had gathered because it was cold outside and there was no cover charge.) The remarkable thing about these gigs from my perspective was that the audiences seemed to be genuinely interested in the content of the songs. This was something I hadn't come across before. At first I thought that these folks were all heavily medicated. This turned out to be mostly true (especially in Cambridge), but it was also true that some percentage of these people were coherent and, unlike my Legion Hall audience, a cup of herb tea and some thoughtful songs actually constituted a good night out for them.

This immediately began to influence my songwriting. Up to that point I had written songs with the wild audience in mind. Discovering this secret society of Saturday night tea drinkers allowed me to unleash a lot of songs that hitherto had no reason to be written.

I continued to do the Don White and Friends shows for four more years while simultaneously becoming a regular on the open mike scene.

During that time I felt like I was straddling two worlds. I can remember the exact moment when I knew I was going to step away from the Legion shows and put all my energy into the coffee house thing. It was a particularly wild Don and Friends Show. I had the drummer introduce me as a pillar of the community. He went on and on about what an upstanding person I was. "Mr. White is a pillar of the community. He's got a *pill-or* a drink in his hands at all times." When he finally got around to introducing me the band kicked into a song called "Junko Partner" that we learned from a Dr. John album. The lyrics tell the story of a man who was inebriated and wobbling down the street. Then I had my friend roll me out from the coatroom in a wheelbarrow with my hair all messed up and a fifth of whiskey in my hand. I crawled up the stairs to the stage with my shirt untucked while the whole band sang about Junko Partner.

After that we went right into a version of a song by Ray Charles called "Let's Go Get Stoned" and ended our opening tribute-to-inebriation trilogy with an up-tempo blues tune by Albert Collins called "I Ain't Drunk, I'm Just Drinking." The audience went wild.

After that initial musical/theatrical glorification of all things intoxicating, and after a couple of pared-down numbers, I found myself on stage alone with my guitar singing a song I had written. It was as if I had said to the audience, "I'm going to sing a tedious folk song now so just use the next five minutes to talk among yourselves and in a few minutes we'll get back to being the cross between the J. Geils Band, the Fools, and a whiskey commercial that you all know and love. Think of this song as an intermission."

There were two hundred people in the room and not one of them (including my family) heard a single word of that song. One minute into it I wished it was over, not just the song but the whole idea of having to light myself on fire to hold the attention of an audience. From the stage I watched my song wander up to and then slink away from each group of people in the room like the nerdy boy in high school who is just realizing that he is invisible to all the cool kids.

While I was singing my little heartfelt song to the accompaniment of one hundred conversations, I was coming to the realization that a person who chose to put his heart out on the table in the West Lynn American Legion Hall on Saturday night would be more than a bit naive if he didn't expect to have that heart handed back to him at the end of the night with a few cigarettes put out in it. "Oh, is this yours? We thought it was an ashtray."

The next day I threw away the mailing list I had assembled from eight years of these shows and I began to focus on the coffee house circuit.

Many of the people that faithfully attended the Don and Friends Shows are very dear friends of mine and I love them. But their idea of a night out in the early nineties was to get hammered, get loud, get laid, and puke—noble endeavors one and all, but likely to acquire turd-in-the-punchbowl status when inserted into the crowd at a church basement coffeehouse.

In order to discourage the fans of my Legion Hall incarnation from following me into my strange new world, I immediately embraced the word folksinger. While some of my contemporaries were distancing themselves from this word, I was seeking refuge in it. It was my secret weapon.

"How come Don doesn't do the Legion Hall shows any more?"

"Didn't you hear? Don became a folksinger."

"Oh, that's so sad. Is it operable? I should send his family a sympathy card."

Telling my existing fans that I had become a folksinger was like telling them that I had joined a monastery. All they could do was let me go and savor the memories. This is called CSS (Cat Stevens Syndrome).

Initially a few of the old guard slipped through my primary folk filter and showed up at my performances. For this group I established a secondary, even more finely meshed filter. I call it my they-don't-serve-any-alcohol-at-my-shows invisible force field. Believe me, to the Saturday night yayhoo community, the folksinger/no alcohol barrier is absolutely impenetrable.

So, while all the other musicians in the world were doing everything in their power to expand their audiences, I was spending an exorbitant amount of time figuring out how to get rid of one that took me eight years to establish.

A few years later this questionable business practice would cause tremendous anguish among some unfortunate persons who had taken on the unenviable job of trying to mold me into something marketable when I employed it to escape a small fan base that had come to me via a two-year internment in the comedy club scene.

Three

The education I acquired from performing in comedy clubs for two years is absolutely invaluable to me. I lean upon those experiences every single time that I perform.

But there came a point while I was experimenting with the possibility of a career in comedy when I began to resent the lack of creative freedom imposed upon comedians by their audience.

Joe Normalguy is walking by the Chinese Restaurant on his way home from work. He sees a handmade sign above the door that says Comedy Tonight. He goes home and tells his wife about it. They attend the show. All night long they laugh heartily at comedians who point out the hysterical differences between how a silly white person and a cool black person will respond to a given situation.

Although they have never been to New York, Mr. and Mrs. N. derive great pleasure from the way the comedians magically morph into stereotypical Brooklyn Italian palookas and grab their nuts when they talk—it's comedy gold. But the most memorable routines —the ones they will be whispering into the ears of their coworkers on Monday—are the ones that deal with the sexual differences between men and women. You see, men are primal and one-dimensional. They don't really love women they just want to fuck them. A man will tell a woman anything he thinks she wants to hear if he believes it will get her to accommodate his life's singular concern. That's funny. Oh, and when a penis talks it has a deep voice and it grunts a lot. When a pussy talks, it has a high-pitched squeaky voice and it wants to know what kind of car you drive.

The second time my fundamental absence of business acumen demanded that I abandon my modest non-folk fan base was around 1992. I had been working as a comic at Catch a Rising Star in Harvard Square for two years. During that time I was also pursuing a folksinger career but I was learning a lot about comedy and giving serious consideration to a career in standup.

Catch was no ordinary comedy club. Because of its unique location at the epicenter of what is arguably the most overeducated two-mile radius on earth, the club could hire the world's most endangered species of mammals: smart comedians.

Robin Hordon hired the talent. His approach to the job was antithetical to all good business sense. He never hired formulaic comedians. He never put together an evening in a way that would make sense—a celebration of women in comedy, three political humorists on the same bill, the all New York, nut-sack-grabbing palooka review. He booked a club in Harvard Square, goddamn it, and he was determined to push the boundaries.

Every Thanksgiving he would hire a Native American comic. He would put together bills that would have a folk-singer, an improv troop, and an edgy political humorist just to see what would happen. He was always trying to get me to play a serious song, as if it was still the early sixties when the clubs in New York would book a poet, a folksinger and a comedian and the beatnik audience would give equal appreciation to each. I tried it once. The audience tolerated it. The world had become compartmentalized. The cold hard truth was that in the nineties, even in the heart of Harvard Square, a comedy club was required by virtue of its name to deliver something at least resembling comedy.

I loved what Robin was doing. I was deeply apprec-iative of the tremendous opportunities that he was giving me. But one day I saw a small blue series of numbers appear on his forehead. It was an expiration date. I knew that his revolutionary spirit was anticorporate and that his tenure in this position at Catch would be relatively short-lived. I asked him about it once and he told me that before he had begun this job he had been one of the air traffic controllers that had been fired by Ronald Reagan for going on strike. "I've been fired by the president of the United States. These people don't scare me." Still I felt like I should learn as much as possible about comedy while he was in a position to provide me the opportunity to study some of the most brilliant and cutting-edge comics of the day.

In those days we would do nine shows in five days— one on Wednesday, two on Thursday, two on Friday, three on Saturday and one on Sunday. I was the emcee. I would do eighteen minutes to start the show and then introduce the regional act. That comic would do thirty minutes. When that set was over I would do another five minutes so people could go to the bathroom before the headliner came on. I would then introduce the national act and he or she would do forty-five minutes.

Every week that I worked I studied attentively as two professional comedians did their act nine times in five days. After the first show I knew where all the punch lines were and I focused in on the mechanics of telling a joke. "Look how this seems like he is making it up off the top of his head every night. Look how he pauses and almost leans forward before delivering that great punch line."

I soaked it all in. I watched as the seedlings of a new joke on Wednesday night grew and blossomed into some-thing hysterically funny over the course of the nine shows. I learned about timing. I learned the difference between knowing that something is funny and saying it in a way that will evoke laughter. I studied the different sounds of laughter and learned to treasure some and disdain others. I watched as comedians dug holes for themselves and studied the different methods they employed to try to dig themselves out. I paid close attention to the different ways that comics dealt with hecklers.

One time I was interviewing Napoleon Duke, a legendary Boston Comic, in front of a classroom of young performers. We were discussing performance skills. I asked him about hecklers, thinking that he would share with the group a couple of methods by which a professional comedian might deal with this common nuisance.

He became very distant. I could see him running through his extensive database of all the mouthy drunks and assholes that he had encountered in his thirty-year career in the clubs. After a moment he looked at me with the deep fatigue of a brilliant artist who had spent a good portion of his career casting pearls before swine and said, "You know, eventually you just learn to hate them."

I got to see a lot of great comedians work in those days.

However, observing a great comic and being one are two entirely different things.

I would be so excited when Robin would call me and say I was on the bill for a week. The biggest reason for my excitement was the money. It paid six hundred dollars. Six HUNDRED dollars! In those days I couldn't tell the difference between the word "hundred" and the word "million."

Four

The person who introduces the folksinger in a coffee house is often a soft-spoken, well-read, globally-conscious Unitarian. She will thank everyone for coming, pull a folded piece of paper from the pocket of her blue jeans, read the names of the other volunteers from the paper, thank each person individually, and give a short description of each volunteer's unique contribution to the event. "I want to thank Jenny LeBlanc who baked a batch of her world-renowned, award-winning chocolate chip cookies for tonight's show. Those cookies as well as brownies and carrot cake will be available during the intermission in the lobby, which is through those big doors to your left."

Eventually, while the audience sits attentively, the host will introduce the artist via some lame quote from that artist's press kit. "And now please join me in giving a big South Street Unitarian Coffeehouse welcome to a singer-songwriter whose music was described in the Worcester Telegram as soulful and relevant—Mr. Jimmy Jones."

After some polite applause Mr. Jones will adjust the microphone stand and strum a G chord. He will then bring his B string into tune, ask Jamie, the volunteer on the sound board, for a little more guitar in the monitor, and then begin to finger pick his first song of the evening—a thoughtful little number about love, life, and the resilience of the human spirit.

The whole process is so low-key that I just nodded off in front of my computer from describing it.

So it's Wednesday night at Catch a Rising Star. It's the first of nine performances. All two hundred seats are full. The audience is young—mostly students from Harvard and MIT. They are pounding down alcohol as if the government had declared that prohibition was to begin at midnight.

I'm standing at the corner of the bar with my guitar. The house lights go down. The stage lights come on. The crowd stops talking and then the intro music begins to blare out of the house sound system. It's Vegas music, like the theme to the tonight show—trumpets, drums and a driving bass line. A voice ten decibels above the music begins my introduction in a style that implies that my journey to the stage will begin by being shot out of a cannon through a burning ring of fire.

"LADIES AND GENTLEMEN! CATCH A RISING STAR IS PROUD TO INTRODUCE YOUR HOST FOR THIS EVENING—AN EXTREMELY FUNNY MAN WHO HAS PERFORMED ALL OVER THE UNITED STATES OF AMERICA—MR. Daw-aw-aw-aw-AW-AWN WHIIITE!"

THUNDEROUS APPLAUSE!

I take the stage. My guitar mike is not set up properly. I pick it up and move it closer to me. I loosen the boom stand and I adjust it so the mike is just a few inches up the neck from the body of the guitar. I move the vocal mike slightly upward toward my mouth and strum a G chord.

I then look up at two hundred power-drinking college students who are staring silently at me and viscerally I realize that I have just squandered all the energy and momentum that my Barnum and Bailey introduction had handed to me.

I tell a one-liner that always got a laugh in the coffee houses. My voice cracks and the crippled punch line falls out of my mouth, hits the front of the stage with a deafening thud and then splatters across the floor like a dropped tray of drinks.

The tidal wave of trepidation that is now consuming my body and mind instantaneously spreads across the room and infects all two hundred people.

It's less than two minutes into my set and it's already hopeless—I am bombing.

In a coffee house situation anything short of stopping in the middle of a song to fall on the floor and whimper in the fetal position would not be considered bombing. Hell, in the coffee houses that embrace the performance poetry community, ending a concert in the fetal position might be considered groundbreaking. Bombing is almost impossible in my folk world.

However, in the comedy scene it is not only possible, it is commonplace. In those days, when I was just a folksinger with a couple of funny songs—when I was just sticking my toes into the waters of the comedy world, the possibility of bombing hung in the air above every crowd salivating and waiting for an opportunity to devour me.

I looked up from the sight of my splattered punch line and someone yelled out "You suck!" Above the stage was a digital clock visible only to the performer. It was there so you wouldn't exceed your allotted time. It read 8:02. I had to fill up sixteen more minutes!

One of the truly diabolical things about bombing is that it dramatically alters time. Think of it as being trapped inside the two-hour minute. I could hear each second as if it were in super slow motion—kaa-lick one, kaa-lick two. I felt like I had been ejected out of an airplane. There was nothing to grab on to. I was just falling with my legs and arms flailing.

Fortunately, I had this here geetar around my neck so I killed five minutes with what was normally a funny song— no laughs tonight though. I blurted out some nervous one-liners, played another song and introduced the next comic five minutes early. I felt as if I had been hit in the head with a baseball bat.

My thirteen-minute set took twenty-five hours. The thirty-minute set that the next comic did took two seconds. When his set was over and I had to stand in front of that group again to kill five minutes, I was not surprised to see that someone had given everyone in the room a musket and turned the audience into a firing squad.

That night I lay in bed staring at the ceiling. I tried to fathom the depths of permanent emotional damage that would be inflicted upon my fragile folksinger psyche by repeating this trauma eight more times over the next four days. I thought about calling Robin and saying that I had been in a car wreck and that I would be in traction for the rest of the week. I considered just not showing up and never setting foot in the building again. All night I mulled over every excuse my mind could come up with to avoid being hurled out of the comedy airplane again but I just couldn't do it. It was two weeks before Christmas and I needed the six million dollars.

The next night I literally ran from the corner of the bar to the stage. Before the applause from my introduction had ended I was delivering my first joke with the conviction of a man possessed—no fumbling with the mikes, no talking to the floor and no squandering of momentum. I squeezed the life out of every millisecond of stage time that night. And the audience responded with giant swells of laughter that felt like warm ocean waves crashing over me. The rest of the week was magical. I had learned the first of many important lessons about the relationship between an audience and a performer—the lesson of who is in control.

Five

One of the last weeks I worked as a comic at Catch I was on the bill with an amazing fellow named Jake Johannsen. His act contained no jokes or one-liners, just brilliant stories with a skewed comic's view of the world that he delivered with a very disarming Midwestern charm. He was from Iowa. As a student of comedy I knew that this was a rare opportunity to study, up close, a truly gifted professional and I did just that. His material was so intelligent that it seemed to be designed specifically for the Harvard Square audience. He had an incredible week. Everyone that attended one of those shows knew that they had witnessed something special.

Those were days when suits from the Catch a Rising Star corporate office were always in the club taking notes and asking questions. "Why is a folksinger on the bill? Who is this guy from Iowa? Doesn't he know any jokes? Is it really a good idea to hire an American Indian on Thanksgiving?" Robin would stand with them by the bar and try to explain his global vision of comedy as a means of accelerating the evolutionary process. The corporate henchmen would move their heads up and down in feigned agreement as if Robin's worldview could somehow alter his fate. It didn't matter what he said. The company had already decided to fire him and these guys had been dispatched to Cambridge to gather enough evidence to justify that decision. Robin's fate had been determined long before their arrival. He knew it and the pulsating blue date on his brow, once almost imperceptible but now visible from across the room, proclaimed it.

I was at another crossroads. I had acquired mediocrity as a comic. It seemed plausible that I could take what I had learned at Catch and scratch out a living in the booming Boston comedy club scene. I had two children and had just bought a house so the fact that comedy clubs, unlike most folk venues, actually guaranteed you a night's pay weighed heavily upon me as I contemplated my future.

The coffee house part of my life at that time was still generating zero dollars but the skills I was acquiring as a comic had filtered into my folk act and were bringing me some recognition. I was becoming known as that funny folksinger.

Initially this distinction separated me from the pack of faceless open mikers and got me a few gigs but I soon found that my ascent into the legitimate folksinger world had quickly reached a plateau and stalled. This forced me to take a hard look at the funny songwriter approach to success in the entertainment world.

Laughter is a convulsion. A person can be predisposed to it but it is involuntary. To get an entire audience into a state of convulsion (not to be confused with a state of revulsion, which is much easier) requires that they do not see the punch line coming.

Here's a joke from Larry the Cable Guy:

"I used to have a job as a lifeguard until some blue kid got me fired."

When you hear the first half of that sentence—"I used to have a job as a lifeguard"—there is no way that you can predict the punch line. It is the element of surprise that causes the convulsion. The second time you hear that joke it might evoke a grin but you will not laugh. And the third time you hear that joke you make a mental note to never pay money to hear it again. Mr. Funny Songwriter was slowly realizing that in order to create a dedicated fan base that would support even a modest career via comedy one would need to be a prolific creator of fresh material.

Unlike the folk world, it is possible to scratch out a living in the comedy clubs without a fan base because Mr.

and Mrs. Normalguy understand what they are getting into when they see the "Comedy Tonight" sign above the door. They know that there will be dick jokes and dick jokes are always funny and therefore always worthy of a cover charge.

If a humorous approach to a discussion of the penis were somehow similarly implied in the word "folk," it is fair to assume that that implication would likely be a much less reliable audience recruitment tool. Aside from songs praising the military-industrial complex, there is nothing more infrequent or more awkward than the recitation of a dick joke before an audience of feminist women and their emasculated husbands in the Unitarian church basement coffee house. (Trust me, I know this.) Put a sign above the door that says "Folk Music Tonight" and see how many people show up. In folk music no fans equals no career.

In those days my coffee house show consisted primarily of humor. (The politically correct non-penis kind, of course.) I did have a couple of songs that were of the emotional variety—the type of songs that my Dad would call tear-jerkers. I had just written one called "I Know What Love Is." It is a long a capella song about the different stages of a woman's life. I would include it in my set but I would never really commit to it. I still believed that audiences were just tolerating these indulgent emotional forays and were impatiently waiting for me to get back to being funny again. So while I was singing one of these serious songs my mind would be all over the place. I'd be thinking, "Is there enough gas in my car to get home? I wonder if the owner will have me back? That guy in the front row hasn't laughed once tonight." I'd be thinking about any and every thing except the song I was singing. I sang "I Know What

Love Is" at every concert. No one ever asked me about it.

One evening I saw some old footage of Judy Garland on television. She was dressed up like a hobo and was sprawled across the stage singing a song. She was pouring every emotional drop of her self into the number. I remember thinking, "This woman has probably been in this play for a month and sings this song every night, yet she is physically feeling every emotion associated with every word as if she was singing it for the first time. What a gift to give an audience—total commitment to the emotional content of the song."

I thought that, at least in the performing arts, this is what constituted greatness—to give the audience complete emotional commitment to every syllable. I thought about Bob Marley. I tried to picture him thinking about the amount of gas in his car while he was singing about the real life struggles of hungry Third World people. It was an absurd thought. When Bob Marley sang, the words, the music and the message were all one thing. He was totally committed to that moment and to me that is one of the qualities that made him great.

The next time I sang "I Know What Love Is" I demanded that my mind shut the fuck up and focus on the feelings that were in the song. I made myself physically feel the emotions as I was singing the words. I emerged from the song as if from a dream—a dream about the important women in my life and how dear they are to me. When I looked around it seemed as if the audience had been pulled up close to the stage. It was as if my commitment to the emotional content of the song had its own gravitational pull. I sold thirty copies of that song during the intermission. Everyone was asking me about it. I knew that every person who bought a CD that night had become a dedicated fan. Nothing would ever be the same for me after that night.

Unlike comedy, the effect of an emotional piece on an audience is not inextricably tied to surprise. Familiarity with the content of a serious song does not diminish the impact on the listener. Not only is the element of surprise not required to accomplish the desired effect but the bulk of the heavy lifting, so to speak, is actually done by the listener. They sit there and wait for you to start the song and then they use the music as a catalyst to bring themselves inside the part of their life experience that connects to the subject matter. Write a good song. Sing it with conviction. And the audience does the rest . . . every single time. To a comic this is almost like cheating.

I had stumbled upon a formula by which my newly acquired comedy skills combined with a few strategically placed emotional songs delivered with conviction were capable of making dedicated fans out of a percentage of every coffee house audience that saw my show.

Six

Sunday was the last night of my week at Catch with Jake Johannsen. The crowd was small—perhaps thirty people. Each group of friends in attendance sat as far away from each other as possible. The audience was a chain of tiny islands in a sea of empty chairs and tables.

Jake began his set with the same astounding stories he had used all week.

Nothing.

Complete silence.

I leaned against the wall at the back of the room and watched as he used a second brilliant story to try to connect with the quiet little islands. I had absorbed every minute of his previous eight performances. I was in awe of his material and his delivery of it. I could recite his whole show word for word and inflection for inflection.

Now I watched as he began to rush his delivery. His timing went out the window and got crushed by a truck on Massachusetts Avenue. Soon he was dragging out material that he hadn't used all week. He was telling a story that was built around drinking beer at a ball game. He started getting some laughs. It was not the deep, rich, oh-my-god-this-guy-is-unbelievable laugh that had filled the room all week. But the suits were happy to hear it. Laughter was laughter to them—but not to me.

To me Jake Johannsen is an artist. What he had done all week for the audiences at Catch a Rising Star was art—no different than that of a great painter or poet or composer.

As I watched him continue to lower the quality of his material to try to find the level of the audience, I began to realize that laughter is a terrible barometer of art. You can make some people laugh with racist humor. People will laugh when they are shocked or embarrassed by what they hear. If you are making your living in comedy clubs you need to fill each and every room with laughter or you don't get to play that room again. Club owners don't give a shit if you are generating quality laughs or racist laughs. They can only tell the difference between a quiet room and a loud room.

So a comedian who has love and respect for comedy and dares to think of it as art is constantly in situations where he or she is forced to dumb it down in order to sustain a living. This realization scared the hell out of me. Having a destiny that is controlled by idiots—that's why God made day jobs. I loved writing songs and entertaining audiences. I dared to call it art. I decided that night to close the door on the possibility of a career as a comic and committed all my energy to developing a career in the folk scene.

It was seven years from that decision before I made another week's pay as a performer.

Part Two
Marlene

By the year 2000 I had developed a small but dedicated fan base. I began to encourage them to hire me for private gatherings. Their willingness to embrace this idea eventually enabled me to make a living in music without becoming an absentee father and husband.

Prior to developing these private performances, I would often drive six hours to some little coffee house in Horse's Ass, New York where, inevitably, no one would come out to see me. The owner of the venue would have the staff and the volunteers sit in the front row as some sort of captive audience/suicide watch. I would be paid one hundred dollars. It would cost at least that much for gas, food and lodging. I would consider the gig successful if it only cost me twenty dollars to do it. That time-honored pearl of wisdom coined by Utah Phillips that says, "In order to make a million dollars in folk music, you need to start out with two million," has its origin in this particular business philosophy.

Occasionally, someone from the suicide watch would feel sorry for me and buy a CD. I have come to refer to these as pity purchases. In the aftermath of these rare and glorious occasions, I would gloat to my friends by telling them that I had done a gig in New York (I'd leave out the Horse's Ass part) and actually broke even.

Eventually my wife sat me down and gave me a little lesson in basic business theory. She grew up in a federal housing project and has brought several interesting character traits from there into her adult personality. The one that reared its lovely head at this business lesson is a dominant one. I call it the Curwin Circle Federal Housing Fundamental Absence of Subtlety.

Just before she spoke, her facial expression sent a telepathic communication to me. It said, "I'm going to say this so even you can understand it." Then she said, "Who the hell runs a business this way? Breaking even is not an accomplishment. Only folksingers, poets and other poor souls, who have completely lost their grip on reality, would boast about not making money. This is a business. It is subject to the same economic laws as every other business. If you owned a pizza place, would you drive to Horse's Ass, New York to sell your pizza?"

So, in what I now see has become a recurring theme, I said goodbye to dozens of fans outside New England. I then empowered my local fans to hire me. I simply told them that if they could create a space where I could have the group's attention, I would consider performing there. Living rooms, back yards, barns, it didn't matter. They responded in some very creative ways. What follows here is one example.

I had done a benefit performance in New Hampshire to raise money for a woman who had cancer and wanted to get some treatments outside the U.S. that her insurance company wouldn't pay for. We raised some money. She got her treatments and perhaps in the big view of things, it bought her some more time to spend with her family. Ultimately, cancer took her.

A few weeks prior to her passing, her family orchestrated a back yard gathering of all her friends and family. I guess you could call it a goodbye Marlene party. I was hired to entertain the guests.

Marlene was very ill. She was on a morphine drip that did, however, allow her to move around without pain. The sun was going down when she emerged from the house. She stood at the top of the stairs by the back door and surveyed this assembly of loved ones—many of whom had traveled long distances to be there. I was looking up at her. The vast twilight sky was her backdrop. The whole situation had a dreamlike feel.

The yard was set up coffee house style. There were several rows of folding chairs facing a makeshift stage against the side of the house. Marlene walked slowly, almost regally, into the back yard and sat in the front row.

Every audience has its own unique personality. Marlene's group had a very complex psychological identity. It was a strange mixture of happiness—friends and loved ones all together—and sadness: "We know that this is probably the last time we will ever see our friend."

Audiences are fickle and difficult to gauge even under normal circumstances. Figuring out this group all of whom were precariously perched between laughing and crying was beyond me. The set was uncomfortable. Every song seemed to have some reference to the future, which was the one thing that was not going to be available in any significant quantity to the guest of honor. I sang a couple of songs that she had requested and my job was done.

Marlene wanted to dance. It was immediately clear to me that it was the best—no, the only—thing that she could do with these moments. If you know that your time in your body is almost over, you really must dance. You must dance with the ones you love. It is the best thing that humans do with their bodies. Lions and tigers seem to have the gift of grace and more than a touch of ballet in every movement. Humans, conversely, often seem gangly and awkward, as if our erectness was an intentional assault on grace itself. I know that my dog is always concerned that the wind might blow me over. He knows that it is extremely dangerous up there and he is constantly at odds with Darwin over the implied infallibility of natural selection. Heated debates on this subject are legendary in the canine science community. However, whenever my dog gains the upper hand in the argument Darwin simply begins to dance. He's quite a good dancer, Darwin. He glides effortlessly around the room and all his detractors are silenced.

At a wedding reception, the father of the bride walks across the empty dance floor. He is tall. He's had a few drinks. The events of the day have accentuated his natural physical awkwardness. His approach is tipsy and teetering. The bride is feeling like she is standing beneath an avalanche of every emotion she has ever known. He takes her by the hand and they begin to dance. At the very instant of their first movement together they become butterflies and everyone in the room is witness to the metamorphosis. These two people are no longer gangly, tipsy, awkward, nervous or overwhelmed. Their dance is a thing of immense beauty— one unified, perfectly choreographed, visual delight, that exists for this moment, one inch off the dance floor, laying claim to the throne of grace and beauty held from time immemorial by the wind in the willows.

If you were somehow able to remain conscious of the world around you after you had left your body, I strongly suspect that you would ache to dance, slowly, with the ones you love.

The sun had gone down. All the folding chairs had been removed. What had just been a concert space was now a dance floor. Marlene put on a recording of Marvin Gaye's greatest hits. As the warm and soulful melodies filled the back yard, she began to move. It was poetry.

I stood back and watched the scene unfold, grateful for these eyes that see so clearly the miraculous in the world around me.

Marlene was bathed in light. It was the light that people walk so willingly toward at the end of their lives. She was a woman between worlds. All the people she had loved encircled her and watched her dance. Her son, a man in his twenties, stepped into her glow. As they waltzed together, Marlene let one hand wave free. Streams of light flew from her fingers and splashed upon faces in the crowd—her sister, her husband, her childhood friend.

The faces, kissed by this light, are difficult to describe. It seemed to me as if she was illuminating these people as they struggled with a thousand contradictory emotions. And their faces, normally a visual indicator of their emotional state, were overwhelmed and short-circuited.

I thought that I might be the one person there with any chance of finding language that could describe the moment. I felt blessed. The next day, with all these extraordinary images still fresh in my mind, I locked myself in my bedroom and did my best to capture the event. What emerged was a song titled "Marlene." I was very proud of the way it turned out, but extremely nervous about how the family would feel about it. I sent a rough cassette copy to them with a note saying that if there was anyone in the family that felt even the slightest bit uncomfortable with it, I would change it so that it would not be associated with their family. I was relieved to hear back from them that they loved it. Marlene actually got to hear it and commented that she had indeed felt like she was between worlds that evening.

Part Three
Dr. Joe

Folksinging is one of the most ridiculous vocations in the world. It is almost impossible to make money at it. If you do, via some extraordinary astrological alignment of planets, become one of the .005 percent of the aspiring artists that manages to get established in the business, it often comes after ten years of poverty and enough personal trauma to put you at the top of the list for a VH1 "Behind the Music" episode. The forces at work against the development of a fan base that is large enough to sustain even a modest career are truly daunting. So much so, in fact, that I am reluctant to list them here without first soliciting the emotional support of a substantial dose of antidepressants. I must confess that it does sometimes seem to me that the world has been designed specifically to bludgeon the creative spirit out of its inhabitants.

Most people are knocked out of the game early on by one, or a combination, of the obvious obstacles: no money, no support, bad contract, too much time away from home, a spouse that was attracted to you because of your creativity and then subsequently became determined to cure you of it, etc. The list is long and not difficult to predict.

I see a world that is populated primarily by poets and painters who, at one time or another, for a myriad of valid reasons, set down their pens and brushes and quietly closed the door on the thing they love.

*****

I was channel surfing yesterday afternoon when I inadvertently clicked into the Dr. Joe Show. Dr. Joe, for those of you who are unfamiliar, is a bald, fat, preachy psychologist who specializes in issues that affect the family. A few years ago, seeing the success that reality TV was having, he put together a daytime television program that brilliantly combined the most popular aspects of reality TV and the Oprah Winfrey Show.

The result was a program that filmed people in their homes and then got those people to view their lives before a studio and a television audience. Dr. Joe would then chastise his guests for their behavior, make them cry, give them advice and get them to promise to evolve into better people. It was an unbeatable ratings formula. It was pure television gold, an instant hit, and must-see TV for millions of conscientious parents.

Yesterday's program featured a glimpse into the life of Mr. and Mrs. Johnson of Missouri—a young couple with three small children. They were in deep emotional turmoil there in front of the good doctor's studio audience because they had just been shown a very unflattering video of their family interactions at home.

The Johnsons wiped tears from their eyes as fat Dr. Joe shook his head from side to side in patent condescension. Meanwhile, the inept and borderline dysfunctional parenting methods of these two middle Americans streamed into millions of living rooms.

The video began with footage that showed the Johnsons completely unable to control their children. Then the kitchen cam showed them in a deep discussion at the table. Mrs. J was saying that she didn't regret for one minute that she had given up her painting when the children were born.

She and her husband had taken the job of parenting very seriously. They knew it would require sacrifices and she was more than willing to put her passion for painting aside because she loved her children and she would do anything for them.

Mr. J agreed (as did the studio audience). He had willingly laid down his acoustic guitar even though, while he was a student at Emerson College in Boston, he had been a regular at the Club Passim open mike on Tuesday nights. The kitchen cam had caught him reminding Mrs. J that several of the volunteers at that legendary folk venue had complimented him on his songs and one of them had told him that his songwriting reminded her of Paul Simon. But still he had placed his guitar in its flimsy case and tucked it away in a corner of the basement on the day their first child was born. It has been collecting dust there ever since—no regrets, he said.

According to everything they had read (and they read everything) on the subject of conscientious child rearing, Mr. and Mrs. J were doing all the right things. They were patient with their children. They took time to explain the complexities of life to them in tedious detail. They employed modern disciplinary methods. Their children had never (God forbid) been spanked. They would instead be given "time outs."

The Johnsons loved the time out. It was the cornerstone of their parenting philosophy. They had come to believe that the time out, when combined with other nurturing parental practices, could stimulate and, in so doing, accelerate a child's natural development of good social skills. The idea is that children are born with the seeds of all the skills necessary to function at a high level in society. The time out simply facilitates the natural growth and development of these skills.

Whenever five-year-old John Junior was behaving in a way that was antisocial, Mom or Dad would isolate him from the rest of the brood. Soon thereafter it was presumed that the magic powers of the time out would force him to objectively view his recent unacceptable behavior. He was expected to use this quiet time to project into the future and envision the cumulative results that this behavior would likely make manifest in him as an adult. Upon seeing this projected image of himself as a twenty-year-old man who fell on the floor and threw tantrums whenever he thought that the other adults weren't playing fair, he would naturally decide to develop better social skills in order to avoid such future embarrassment.

For the Johnsons and millions of other good parents, the time out was an indispensable child-rearing tool. All they had to do was to physically separate the child from the scene of his or her antisocial behavior and provide a quiet place that encouraged contemplation. The time out would do the rest.

However, after several years of dutiful adherence to,

and the patient application of, the time out, Dr. Joe's video was now proving that the Johnsons' children were still what my mom would call little bastids.

Dr. Joe stood up, faced the camera, and prepared to deliver a lecture designed specifically to devastate his guests by systematically dismantling and thereby invalidating their treasured child rearing doctrine.

Before Dr. Joe spoke, the producer of the show, who had seen a draft of the lecture, leaned over to a cameraman and whispered into his ear, "I smell an Emmy."

I feel that it is important to note here that although Dr. Joe is extremely manipulative, incurably ambitious, and, in truth, completely insensitive to the plight of the guests on his show, he is not stupid. He is smart—very, very smart. What he is about to say to this young couple is thoughtful and concise and should they choose to apply his advice to their problems, that application is likely to significantly enrich their lives. Dr. Joe is always right. He is also always what my Mom would call a son of a bitch, because, as Mom well knows, being right and being a prick are two things that are not mutually exclusive.

Let me ask you a question.

What would *you* call someone who was in possession of specific knowledge that could dramatically improve your quality of life but will only reveal it to you if you let him tear you to shreds in front of millions of people so he can reap the harvest of high ratings first?

Dr. Joe addressed the Johnsons by their first names. He did so, interestingly enough, while looking into the camera. He acknowledged and praised their commitment to their children and then he began his lecture.

"Children are interesting little creatures," he said. "They

never really comprehend the reason why you are telling them to do or not to do something. That capability is beyond the immediacy of their worldview.

"Let's say that you want to encourage good oral hygiene in your young daughter. You may choose to do so by using the conscientious parent method—you patiently explain to her that in order to keep one's teeth white and shiny, one must brush them vigorously after every meal. Or perhaps you are a few links lower on the parental food chain, and patient, detailed explanations are not your forte. So you do what comes naturally—you make up a lie that you think will scare the child into establishing and maintaining good dental practices. 'If you don't brush your teeth, you'll turn into a gorilla.'

"Both the tedious conscientious method and the expeditious unscrupulous one are equally ineffective because they are each based on the fallacy that children can comprehend the concept of the future. The future is for grown-ups. Now! Now! Now! That is for children. Trying to make a person do something today because it will benefit them ten years from now, when that person has absolutely no concept of what ten years means, is always ineffective.

"It is very important that you understand that children absorb your methods, not your message.

"If you use the you'll-turn-into-a-gorilla trick on your daughter, you are teaching her the method you use to get someone to do what you want them to do. This is tremendously useful knowledge for her because it can be applied immediately in her daily struggles. You will never see a child telling another child about the long-term benefits of good oral hygiene, which was the intended goal of the gorilla trick. There is, however, an excellent chance that one day you will hear your daughter telling her playmates that if they don't share their toys with her, they will all turn into gorillas.

"What I want you two to do now is to visualize a world where well-intentioned, conscientious parents like you folks are carefully articulating all the details of life's important lessons to their children. Then picture those children looking up at their parents with no ability to comprehend what is being said. While the mouths of the adults move up and down emitting the equivalent of gibberish, these children are viscerally incorporating into their own personalities the body language, vocal inflections, and all the other assoc- iated minutiae that their parents employ to manipulate someone into doing what they want them to do.

"Now John, you used to write songs and play guitar when you were in college. I'm told you were very good. And your stressed-out wife over there, she used to write poetry and paint, isn't that true? So, how come you guys don't do those things anymore? Oh, I see. Once you had children you quit all that stuff because you are both very conscientious parents and you needed more time to sit down and articulate all the details of life's many lessons to your little cherubs. How's that working out? Are they getting it—you know, all that stuff about how what they do now affects the way it will be for them in the future?

"Let's try looking at this a different way. Let's say that when you martyr your creativity on behalf of your children, you're teaching them that they should martyr their own. Let's also assume that one of the interesting unintended effects of this noble martyrdom might be the guilt associated with the knowledge that Mom and Dad would have been doing what they love if only I had never been born.

"Let's also, for the sake of argument, assume that that

dreadful cliché 'live by example' actually is valid and can apply to child rearing."

Dr. Joe was in the zone. This was going to be the highest-rated episode ever. In his mind he could see tears of empathy rolling down the cheeks of millions of stay-at-home moms from coast to coast. All he had to do was wrap this up with compassion and a recipe for positive change and he could go home tonight and write his acceptance speech for that Emmy.

The producer of the show told the cameraman to zoom in on Dr. Joe. On cue the good doctor turned toward the camera. His huge, puffy face was now consuming the entire screen on millions of televisions in America. Even people who had the TV on but were not watching found themselves frozen in place. "Whoa, look at that gigantic head on my TV."

Joe was very focused. He had systematically unraveled the emotional well-being of these people before a national audience. He had pointed out that the noble relinquishing of their personal dreams would, in all likelihood, cause their children to eventually give up on their own dreams. He had done this knowing that these people loved their children more than anything in the world and that nothing would cause them deeper emotional pain than realizing that they had unwittingly all but guaranteed that the dreams of their children would not come true.

He also knew that after having completely broken them, he needed to put them back together because greatness in the mediocre world of television is gauged by overcoming adversity—even if that adversity is manufactured deliberately so that it might later be overcome for the sake of ratings.

The lips on the giant head that had been thrust into

the homes of America began to move.

"My friends, if you'll bear with me, I'd like to talk about human development and how we as a species are different in very important ways from all the other creatures on earth.

"Early man was not blessed with the strength of a lion or the swiftness of the gazelle. Nor was he given wings to fly. He could not overpower, outrun, or fly from danger. His survival depended upon community. One man alone in the jungle was no match for a hungry lion, but ten men with spears could bring down an elephant.

"When human children are born, they need years of care and nurturing if they are to survive to adulthood. In the early days of our development as a species, when we were considered something of a delicacy by many of our neighbors in the animal kingdom, the survival of the tribe depended upon the contributions of every person in it. We needed each other. Our lives depended on each other.

"Although modern society allows us to live much more independent lives, every single baby that is born carries within a genetic need to contribute to the tribe. We still need to feel that what we do is useful. I've done a lot of work over the years with people who are clinically depressed. You'd be amazed at the kind of progress these folks make when they are able to do something that is helpful for other people. There is an emptiness inside a lot of people that is just waiting to be filled by a sense of being useful—by being of value, if you will. It doesn't have to be global. You don't have to win a Nobel prize for what you do. Quite the contrary, it can be as simple as giving a lonely person someone to talk to. It can come from taking pride in your work or from just being a good friend to someone."

Dr. Joe turned toward the Johnsons as the camera pulled back and revealed their devastation to his television audience.

"John and Mary, I know this has been hard for you. You've been very courageous to come here and talk to America about the challenges facing your family, and I want to thank you very sincerely for that. I also want to take a few minutes to tell you how special you are and how optimistic I am about your future.

"Things look bad now but I've got to tell you that I think you two are uniquely positioned to turn this around because, unlike most people in the world, you both know what you love to do. Most people never even allow themselves to think about what they love. But *you* know that you love writing songs and playing guitar, and *you* know that you love to paint.

"The one thing that we have all learned about you two is that you are willing to do anything humanly possible to ensure that your children have every opportunity to fulfill their dreams. Well, I'm here to bring you the good news that all you have to do to make that a reality is to get back in touch with your own dreams. You just have to approach it differently than you have done in the past. Don't think of it as a career. Just think of it as a way to stay connected to your inner voice. Think of it as a time for meditation. Think of it as a way to show your children that it is normal to figure out what you love in this world and to budget time into every day of your life to do it.

"John, tomorrow when you come home from work I want you to let your wife and children know that you are going into the basement for thirty minutes to practice your guitar because that is what you love to do. Then do it.

When you are finished, I want you to take over the dinner preparations and let Mom go downstairs to paint for thirty minutes. When she is finished the two of you have to do the one thing that is almost impossible for well-intentioned, dedicated young parents to do—you need to NOT talk about it.

"If you demand a reasonable amount of time in your day to do the thing that you love without neglecting your responsibilities to the family, your children will grow up knowing that that is normal. You don't have to explain it to them. You just have to do it. Children learn from what you do, not from what you say. I know that you want the best for them. Isn't it nice to know that what is best for your own mental health is what is best for theirs?

"The arts—whether it be writing, singing, sculpting, painting, woodworking, dance, theatre or any other creative endeavor—are a direct link back to our genetic need to contribute to society. All art has some meditative value for its creator, but its real potential value is in the giving of it to the world.

"By embracing the creative part of your lives you will be feeding and nurturing your spiritual center. You will be teaching your children to do the same. Nothing you can say to them will have more of a lasting effect on their overall well-being than this.

"Remember, you are not necessarily pushing them toward a career in the arts. You are showing them a wonderful process through which they can release the pressures of modern life. You are teaching them how to take care of themselves."

Looking into the camera Dr. Joe said, "Those of you at home who have never allowed yourselves to even think about what you would love to do, who never believed that you had anything to offer the world, I want you to begin today to give it some serious thought.

"Those of you who dabble in or used to dabble in an expressive art form of any kind, I encourage you to do it. Don't worry about making money at it. Just do it. Do it every day. Get good at it. Use it as a refuge. Use it to maintain your mental health. The least that will happen is that you will be the one person in a thousand that stays connected to his or her creative voice. And maybe, somewhere along the line, you—or even better, one of your children—might just be the one person in a situation who can articulate and, in so doing, capture with love and compassion, and contribute to the tribe, the poetry of a beautiful moment in time.

"We'll be back after this short commercial break to discuss tomorrow's show, where we'll sit down with Mr. and Mrs. Wellstone of Kansas and their fifteen-year-old daughter who is addicted to crack and having a sexual relationship with her stepfather. Don't go away."

*****

They all came here just to see Marlene.
No more doctors, no more treatments now, just friends and family.
When she walks into the back yard, you can see it on her face.
Marlene is where the Hospice people call the sacred place.

They circle her as music starts to play.
She is dancing like an angel to a song by Marvin Gaye.
Marlene is not quite here. Marlene is not quite gone.
She's dancing somewhere between this yard and the great big blue beyond.

Marlene can see the light that shines out from the other side.
That light is all around her now. That light is in her eyes.
It flies off of her fingers as she dances with her son.
And it splashes on the faces of these people that she loves.

They all came here just to see Marlene.
Soon they will all go home and think over these things that they have seen.
I think all that she is saying is, "Make time for those you love."
As she dances between worlds here in the back yard with her son.

Marlene can see the light that shines out from the other side.
That light is all around her now. That light is in her eyes.
It flies off of her fingers as she dances with her son.
And it splashes on the faces of these people that she loves.

She is lighting up the faces of these people that she loves.

My Terrorist Experience

If you bring a person from my hometown of Lynn, Massachusetts, into an empty restaurant and say, "Sit wherever you want," that person will likely choose the seat that is furthest from the door with its back to the wall and a full view of the room. This speaks volumes about who we are and the world that we know.

For several weeks after terrorists destroyed the World Trade Center, there was a lot of talk about America having lost her innocence. Americans had been made aware, in no uncertain terms, that they were not immune to sudden acts of violence.

As the press continued to promulgate this image of a country where, prior to September 2001, the citizens were free from terrorism, I began to wonder what country I had been raised in. I called my mother. "Hi Ma, where did I grow up?" "Oh Donnie, are you back on drugs again?" "No Ma, just tell me what country I grew up in." "You grew up in America, honey."

She was mistaken. I could not have been raised in America because my innocence was not lost in September of 2001. It was lost in July of 1962—the day I met my first terrorists.

I was five years old. My mother and I had walked to my aunt's house. The two of them were sitting at the kitchen table smoking and talking. My mother called me in from the yard, gave me a dollar and sent me to Tarr's Pharmacy for a pack of Winston cigarettes. I put the money in my pocket and headed out on my tricycle. I wasn't sitting on it. I was using it the cool way where you lean over and hold the handlebars, keep one foot on the rear runner and push with the other foot.

Tarr's Pharmacy was at the far end of a long urban industrial block. On one side of the street was a meat packing plant. On the other side was the parking lot for the West Lynn General Electric factory. In retrospect, I see it was a neighborhood that was very conducive to terrorist activity.

I was cruising along on the sidewalk near the parked cars when a voice called out to me. "Hey kid, come over here." Being five and having never met a terrorist before, I perceived no impending trauma and pushed my bike into the parking lot. There behind a van, which blocked the view from the street, stood three kids—two tall ones (compared to me) and one my size. The tallest one asked me where I lived and some other questions and then, without warning, the small one hauled off and slapped me across the face. Whap! Innocence gone. Then he ran away. As I stood there crying, the remaining two terrorists took turns supplying me with all the information I would need to locate their recently departed associate in case I ever felt inclined to deliver unto him a degree of retribution befitting the crime that he had just perpetrated upon me. They told me his name and where he lived. They actually gave me detailed directions on how to find the apartment house that he lived in, the color of the building and what floor he lived on. They didn't take my dollar or my bike. They just conspired to terrorize me and then to rat out their friend.

This was my initiation into the world around me. A world where no logic need apply, where acts of violence were not unduly encumbered by a need for superficial justification, where being weak was justification aplenty. On this warm day in July of 1962 I had begun my journey to adulthood in a world where having the seat against the far wall with a full view of the room was a matter of survival. I called it America. Apparently I was mistaken.

Six years later, I was a short, skinny, eleven-year-old seventh grader. I was walking home from Breed Junior High School one afternoon with the sun behind me when I saw three large shadows appear simultaneously on the sidewalk before me. The shadows were attached to three fifteen-year-old seventh graders. They were all members of that special group of students who will never make it to high school. The final page of the public educational experience for these teenagers is usually written somewhere around the time of their sixteenth birthday after they have been kept back for the fourth consecutive time and are five years older than most of the other kids in their class.

It is reasonably safe to assume that a seventh grader's scholastic career is winding down when he has a beard and is driving his own car to school.

Because I had just barely gotten promoted from the sixth grade, I was put in the class with these perennial seventh graders. The class was called 7-I. At Breed Junior

High School in the sixties the seventh, eighth, and ninth grades were each broken up into ten groups. Each of these groups was given a letter from A to J. If you were destined for college, you were in A, B, C, or D. The business students were assigned to E, F, G, or H. My community, 7-I and 7-J, was essentially a containment area for everyone else.

Breed School was two buildings. There was a newer building called the Annex and the original building, which had been built in 1906. The older building was where they attempted to contain the students in 7-I and 7-J.

The floors creaked. The stairs were made of metal. The glass in the doors that swung open to the stairwells had been broken so often that the administration had begun using a special type of replacement glass that had chicken wire inside it. These windows would still be routinely broken intentionally by students, but the chicken wire would hold the pieces together and keep them from spraying down the corridor.

A hard punch to the center point of these windows would create a ragged six-inch circle indentation from which cracks would extend to each of the four corners of the frame, thus creating a piece of contemporary urban art, a social statement depicting the sun (center of the universe) and the magnificence with which its light shines equally upon all creatures good and evil. One could often observe the creator of such a masterpiece admiring his work and wondering aloud about the inherent shortcomings of an educational system where a young artist, capable of such creative depth, could so consistently fail art class.

The desks and chairs had been there since 1906. They each had cast iron bases that were bolted to the floor. The school administration began replacing them in 1969 with the non-stationary type after the class of 7-J discovered that the structural integrity of the classroom floor could be significantly compromised if everyone rocked back and forth at the same time in their bolted-down chairs.

The desks were made of wood. Each one had a hole in the top right corner that had once held an inkwell. The tops were engraved with witticisms from previous generations of West Lynn adolescents. These pearls of wisdom were often carved so deeply into the wood that you would have to place your work paper on whatever section had the shallowest carvings so your pencil wouldn't fall into a crater and tear your paper. When I use the term "shallowest," I'm referring to the actual physical depth that the jack knife had penetrated the wood. I think it would be fair to say that all the literary content of these etchings fell well within the term "shallow." "Eat me." "This place sucks." "Colleen is a doosh bag." Not a lot of profundity here.

The boys' room was a testimonial to nineteenth-century engineering. Each toilet had a pull chain that would release water from a holding tank above the stall. There were no urinals. Instead there was a six-foot high, ten-foot long wall of slate—a piss wall. It had a thin perforated copper pipe running horizontally across the top. From the holes in this pipe small steady streams of water sprayed out and kept the piss wall wet. At the base of the wall was a small trough with a drain at one end. Urinating in the old Breed boys' room was a social event, a group endeavor. Ten young men lined up shoulder to shoulder whipping it out and pissing on the wall, over the wall, and at each other.

Everyone in 7-I and 7-J had one thing in common: bad grades. But aside from this lack of scholastic achievement, we were a fairly diverse group. There were some good-natured slow kids who would now be diagnosed with learning disabilities, but in the sixties were just called stupid. There were the quiet kids who had a home life that was so messed up that they were just not capable of concentration. There was also a group of six or seven really tough girls.

This was my first exposure to young women whose destiny included significant jail time. They were always late for class. I suspected that their perpetual tardiness was intentional because they so loved to make the big entrance. These young ladies all had a God-given natural talent for drama.

"Miss Jones you're late again. Don't sit down. Just go straight to the principal's office." Miss Jones ignores him, brushes off his commands like an insect from her shoulder and sits at her desk. This may be the only few moments this month that Mr. Lewis will have the undivided attention of his entire student body.

As a group we place our elbows on our desktops, lean forward, rest our faces into our open palms, and watch intently as the familiar scene unfolds. Mr. Lewis repeats his command. Before he is half finished, Miss Jones lifts up her desktop and hides her head behind it. I am beside her and I can see by her face how thoroughly she is enjoying both ignoring Mr. Lewis and the attention it has brought her. He walks to her desk. He shuts the desktop and in so doing accidentally touches her shoulder.

OK boys and girls, now it's *show time*.

She leaps out of her seat, and with the head-bobbing swagger invented and perfected by seventh grade tough girls, she screams, "Don't you touch me! Don't you EVER touch me! Who the hell do you think you are?" He repeats his command for her to get out of his class. With every eye in 7-I fixed upon her, she struts to the exit, sweeps a stack of math books off a table en route, slams the door behind her, and disappears into the hallway.

We are ready to give a round of applause and a standing ovation to Miss Jones for her performance, but the beet-red face of Mr. Lewis, counterbalanced by a throbbing blue vein at each temple, warns us against it. I remember thinking that whoever had the good fortune to marry the lovely Miss Jones could expect to see a grown-up version of this performance played out upon occasion in a restaurant or two during the course of his marriage.

And then there were the tough guys. Guys like Glen Stevens (fifteen years old, but he could easily have passed for twenty). Glen was a giant. He could barely fit in his seat. Seeing him sitting at his desk always called to mind the circus image of a gorilla on a tricycle. This was his third and final shot at the seventh grade and school in general. He was the uncontested heavyweight champion of grade seven and the king of 7-I.

Henry Baker (also fifteen). He was the most recent of several memorable gifts to the public school system, and to society at large, from a legendary family of multi-generational West Lynn criminals. His old man and one of his brothers were both in jail. He was greasy and incurably dishonest. He had dark eyes that avoided eye contact as if it were encoded into his DNA. You always had the feeling that he was studying you when you weren't looking. When you did look at him you would only see his eyes darting away. He was a thief, a burglar and, like Mr. Stevens, a third-year seventh grader.

Jamie Henderson (thirteen, but as tall as Glen). He loved to hang around with the tough guys but he seemed to lack their intestinal fortitude.

Guys like Glen and Henry had wills of steel. There was absolutely nothing that anyone in authority could threaten them with that was more intimidating than what they were accustomed to dealing with at home.

One time we were in a study period on the third floor of the old building. The teacher was late. An unsupervised environment with this cast of characters always engendered a palpable sense of excitement. You knew something criminal was about to happen. As the seconds ticked away and no person of authority arrived, there was no doubt that this day would soon be transformed from just another indistinguishable series of heavily policed group movements between classes to a classic episode of crime and punishment and a textbook lesson in sociology. The question was not *if* a crime would be committed but rather *what* ingenious new illegal activity would the great criminal minds of our generation create to best utilize the fortuitous blessing of these precious moments.

The question was soon answered.

There were no lockers in the old building. Consequently, any books that students were not carrying upon their persons were left inside the desks to which they were assigned in their homeroom—the very desks that were presently being occupied by the wayward adolescents in my class, the great unwatched.

The apprehension in the room ended when Glen drew every eye to him by opening the top of the desk that he was crammed into. There before him lay a treasure trove of fodder for his brilliant and unprecedented new adventure in juvenile delinquency. He grabbed an armful of textbooks, walked over to an open window and hurled them out. It was raining. The books dropped like bricks and hit the puddles in the pavement with a splat. When this sound reached our third floor window, it proclaimed, "Let the games begin!"

A half dozen perennial seventh graders immediately joined the festivities. In the classroom below, Mr. Lewis was groaning on about one of the many interesting nuances of long division when he thought he saw a book drop past his window. "Must have been a bird," he thought. But when it happened again, he knew it was not a bird. It was a math book. Algebra One—he'd know it anywhere. He went to the window and hung his head out in order to verify his suspicions and was nearly decapitated by a Webster's dictionary. As dozens of middle school textbooks rained past his class and piled up in a soggy heap in the school-yard, he dashed out of the room and ran upstairs. He believed in his heart that when these miscreants ran out of books, they might very well start hurling smaller seventh graders out the window. As one of these potential hurlees, I was secretly very thankful for his arrival.

When he entered the room, frantic and out of breath, we were all sitting at our desks with our hands folded. If he had not just been witness to our reckless destruction of school property, he might very well have thought that he had crossed a time barrier and stumbled into a parallel universe. A world where the alter egos of young criminals had been waiting patiently in their assigned seats for the belated arrival of their beloved teacher.

We were a hands-folded, backs-straight-and-tall, forward-facing, extremely cynical, mock manifestation of every junior high school teacher's wet dream. In my memory I see this scene in black and white, as if it were from an episode of

Ozzie and Harriet. I almost expected to see Henry Baker raise his hand and ask permission to approach the teacher's desk to give him an apple he had polished himself as a gift from the class to show their appreciation for the extraordinary educational experience they were receiving.

Mr. Lewis was not impressed. He surveyed the room, and without saying a word, he left.

In the quiet of his absence, a frightening realization began to take form. We were all familiar with criminal activity; it was, after all, our occupation. We were also aware that criminal activity came in many shapes, sizes, and depths of gravity. For example, stuffing up the drain at the base of the piss wall with paper towels and causing it to overflow was a kind of misdemeanor, a call-your-mother crime. But hundreds of 1969 dollars-worth of taxpayer-financed schoolbooks, soaking in a camera-friendly pile in the schoolyard was a kind of felony—a call-your-police-chief crime.

When Mr. Lewis returned, he was accompanied by the principal, the vice-principal, and two guidance counselors. The entire disciplinary hierarchy of Breed Junior High School was now conducting military maneuvers off the coast of 7-I in a show of strength and intimidation. The playful mock innocence that Mr. Lewis had previously encountered was gone. This was serious. This wasn't going to end with a couple of kids getting detention. This situation had a good chance of culminating with someone getting expelled and being prosecuted in court. We were now at war.

A quick perusal of the facts of this case might easily lead a person to believe that it should be resolved in short order and with relative ease. You have a serious crime witnessed by thirty students in a class whose test scores clearly predict a future in the unskilled manual labor segment of America's workforce. How hard could it be for a college-educated vice-principal to trick, coerce, or scare the truth out of one of them?

However, if anyone had taken the time to develop a clear understanding of the complexities of survival in this environment, they would soon conclude that a witness testimony, coerced or otherwise, is a very rare bird in this part of the world.

The first official act of the tribunal was to round up the usual suspects. They took Henry into the vice-principal's office for interrogation. This quickly proved to be a colossal waste of time. People do not turn out to be Henry Baker by accident. They are the products of a home life that borders on the unspeakable. All of the threats that might elicit a confession from a lesser seventh grader were completely incapable of penetrating the battle-hardened armor of the young Mr. Baker.

The vice-principal is looking through a folder that contains Henry's lengthy disciplinary record. When he looks up from the paper and across his desk, he catches a fleeting split second of eye contact. These are the eyes of a predator, he thinks. They are perfectly designed to see through any facade to the weakness it is concealing. As he recites his standard list of threats, his mind is secretly running through the reasons why they are all useless in this situation. Henry Baker and all the others like him have been schooled in the fine art of intimidation (both the resisting and imposing of it) by the best in the business. They know when you are bluffing.

After getting nowhere with the tough kids, they turned

to what they considered a sure bet—the not-so-tough kids. They took us into the principal's office one at a time. They sat me in a chair and then the principal, the vice-principal, and two guidance counselors encircled me. This psychological maneuver has come to be known colloquially as the cluster fuck. It was high-pressure intimidation.

First the vice-principal told me that they already knew who had committed the crime and that they were just giving me a chance to help myself by telling the truth. Then the guidance counselor on my left leaned in close enough so I could smell his breath and that late-afternoon, possibly carcinogenic, mixture of cheap cologne and perspiration. He told me that he knew I was a good kid and that they would be talking to everyone individually so no one would ever know who identified the perpetrators. I had become the central figure in a scene from a mediocre television police drama.

While all this was going on I kept remembering the sound of biology books slapping against wet pavement. I thought to myself that it was probably not a lot different from the sound a person's head would make when it was being slammed against the piss wall.

Although I am certain that the cluster fuck had a long and storied history of success at Breed Junior High School, it had virtually no chance of eliciting information from anyone in my class. The fact that the administration believed that it could exposed a basic lack of appreciation for the magnitude of the social and survival issues we encountered and dealt with on a daily basis. The scholastic history of the eleven-year-olds in my class may very well have indicated that we were borderline imbeciles, but when it came to staying alive in our world we were all geniuses. Within the arena of survival, we were like the little weak kid Mensa society. None of us could tell you the difference between a comma and a semicolon if we had all day to answer with the book opened to the page that explained it. But there was no situation imaginable that could possibly keep us from knowing the difference between a terrorist and a paper tiger.

Despite all their clever psychological tactics and bad breath, the school administration could not change one basic fact: they were prohibited from killing us. It's in their bylaws. "You may threaten, coerce, lie, and subject them to cheap cologne, but at no time is it permissible to kill them."

When the vice-principal dismissed me from his interrogation, he was sending me back to a community where no such restrictions existed.

*****

Back on Cottage Street, the terrorists attached to the three shadows that appeared on the sidewalk before me were Glen, Henry, and Jamie. As they encircled me, I became overwhelmed by a deep sense of empathy for the mouse that my cat had dragged into the kitchen the night before. Glen slid his hands under my arms, lifted me off the sidewalk and threw me to Jamie. My books and papers went sailing into traffic. The three of them proceeded to toss me like a football to each other as they walked home. Periodically they would incomplete a pass. As a result I was bounced off a parked car, a telephone pole, and a tree. To add an additional sense of fun and excitement to their new game (which was quite possibly the original inspiration for dwarf tossing), they would spit on me between passes.

Unfortunately for me, what these guys called spitting was in actuality an enterprise much more disgusting than that term would indicate. There was no saliva involved. This stuff came from their lungs. They would make this low gurgling sound and conjure up, from deep inside their beings, this green-yellow glob. They would curl it up in their tongue and it would hurl out of them with an unmistakable thupping sound.

When they were dwarf tossing you down the street, they were establishing complete dominance over you while simultaneously implanting into the core of your being a permanent sense of terror. When they were spitting on you, they were poisoning the soil around any seedling of dignity that might survive the ordeal and foolishly try to grow in the future.

Eventually they dropped me on the sidewalk and strolled off toward Barry Park.

Twenty minutes later I walked into the kitchen of our house on Abbott Street. I was disheveled, red-faced, humiliated, beat up, and spat upon. My mother asked me what had happened. I told her the story, ending it in my Boston accent with the sentence "and they hucked a buncha lungas on me too, Ma."

She was very calm and methodical. The look on her face was one of controlled anger. She asked me if I knew the names of the perpetrators. I did. She asked me if I could point them out. I could. Then, just prior to her getting up from the table and walking over to the phone, she gave me a look that said, "Trust me, this is the last time this is going to happen to you."

Now it had never occurred to my three terrorists that my family hadn't just moved to Lynn from the suburbs. I am, in fact, a third-generation direct descendant of the founding fathers of West Lynn juvenile delinquency. My bloodline had invented and subsequently perfected much of the behavior to which I had just been subjected. There was something unmistakable in my mother's walk to the phone that bespoke a personal familiarity with this type of incident and a clear understanding of exactly what actions were necessary to ensure that it would never happen again.

I sat in the kitchen and listened in as she called her friend from the next street over. "Hi Mary. Listen, Donnie just came home from school. Some older kids beat him up. Yeah. They hucked a buncha lungas on him too—the little shits. Listen, could you let Gary know about it for me? You could? Thanks Mare, I appreciate it. Talk to you later."

At this point, dear reader, I assume that you are speculating as to who Gary might be. Perhaps you're thinking Mary was married to the principal of the school and her husband Gary could address this situation by assembling a meeting between all the parents of the students involved? Or maybe Mary's husband Gary was a police officer, and might be persuaded to apply the pressure of the law upon these kids?

Wrong and wrong again.

Gary was my babysitter.

Every Saturday night my parents would go out. One hour later, unbeknownst to them, our house would be the scene of a huge party. There would sometimes be twenty intoxicated teenagers there. There would be fistfights, cases of beer, and people puking out the back door. Many nights my brother and I would be able to stay up really late because Gary's buddies would have their girlfriends in our beds. We loved it. To us he was simply the greatest babysitter of all time.

Gary was in high school and he was very tough. He was the real thing. He was destined to move on, and live a life that included a little jail time, but in 1969 he was one of a handful of people in the city who could absolutely guarantee that your walk home from school would be problem-free. My mother, bless her heart, had for all intents and purposes just hired a hit man.

The next day Gary was waiting in the corridor when we were released from class for lunch. He escorted me outside the building to a window that looked down into the cafeteria. He was with one of his friends from high school—a very large teenager that I recognized from a particularly exciting Saturday night brawl in my kitchen. He asked me if I could see any of the junior terrorists. I scanned the cafeteria and pointed out Jamie Henderson, who was sitting at the end of a table near the door. Gary told me to wait there while he went into the cafeteria. I watched through the window as he walked over to Jamie and whispered something into his ear. Jamie got up and the two of them left the cafeteria. Soon they were walking toward me in the schoolyard.

At the exact moment Jamie recognized me, Gary's friend appeared on his opposite side and took hold of his arm. Jamie's face became flushed with the same fear that he and his friends were accustomed to seeing on the faces of the kids that they drop kicked to each other on the way home from school. Gary and his friend escorted poor Jamie to where I was standing like two boy scouts helping an old woman across the street. Gary's friend held Jamie's arms behind his back. Gary pointed to me and said, "You see this kid? If you touch him again, you're dead." Then he hauled off and slapped him across the face. Whap! Dominance established. It was a vicious slap. One side of Jamie's face turned bright red. In the brief silence that followed, an immediate and permanent reconfiguration of the pecking order at Breed Junior High School was established. I was no longer at the bottom and Jamie and his friends were no longer at the top. One open-hand slap to the face of a junior high school terrorist from the hand of a high school terrorist officially closed the door on my tenure as a person who could be tormented with impunity.

*****

A few months after I graduated from high school in 1974 I began a hitchhiking adventure around North America that would consume the bulk of the next five years. This was the time in my life where I sought out all the people and situations that were as far away as possible from what I had grown up around.

I hitchhiked to Alaska. I read about Buddhism. I visited ashrams. I learned about the Baha'i faith. I lived in communal situations with hippies who exposed me to yoga and meditation. I became a vegetarian. Every day during these years I was exposed to new ideas that expanded my view of the world.

I became philosophical.

In adulthood, neither of my distinct identities has succeeded in eliminating the other. They exist within me for the good of the whole, with the same respect and animosity that exists in theory between a Democratic president and a Republican congress. As long as Brickyard Don perceives no physical or psychological threat, he is quite content to let

Philosopher Don do all the talking. Brickyard Don has become a sort of bodyguard.

For instance, when we go out to eat, he demands that we sit with our back to the wall with a full view of the room. While Hippie Don ponders the institutionalized economic oppression of the waitress and the busboy, Brickyard Don watches the room for any behavior that might pose a threat.

One day I was walking along Massachusetts Avenue in Harvard Square in Cambridge when a man asked me how to get to Harvard University. I perceived no threat. Hippie Don (sometimes called Mouthy Don) was at the helm. He waved my arm in a circle and said, "Everything you see here is Harvard University." My unintentional glibness instantly unleashed the severe mental illness that boiled just beneath the surface of this man's countenance. He responded to me as if I had told him that I had just finished raping his sister the nun. He got right up in my face and began screaming, "You motherfucker! I will rip your fucking head off right here, right now."

An emergency conference between the two Dons was called.

Hippie Don: Should I turn the face over to you?

Brickyard Don: No. This guy is crazy, not tough. If I throw my I'm-a-bad-ass face up here it is not going to work the same as if we were dealing with a mugger who was trying to get our money with the least amount of resistance. Muggers are rational. I've told you this before —in a fight, crazy beats tough every time.

HD: Well then, I think it's time for you to let me in on Plan B because I think we're seconds away from violence here and you know that I am philosophically against violence, especially when it is happening to me.

BYD: You are such a pussy. OK, you're going to do the opposite of what he expects. He's expecting you to hit him. You could hit this guy with a lead pipe and he wouldn't feel it. There is nobody home in there. We can't win this one that way. I want you to surrender.

HD: Surrender?

BYD: Yes, drop all the resistance and indignation from your face. Replace it with remorse and a willingness to repent. Then apologize to him. Tell him that he has every right to be angry and that you should not have been so arrogant and flippant to him. Then tell him that what you should have said was that Harvard owns almost all of the buildings in Harvard Square so if he is looking for the main information area, it is over there to the left across the street.

Hippie Don does this perfectly and the man is instantly disarmed. It was as if we had replaced his enemy with someone who needed his help to learn how to be a better person.

While this metamorphosis was taking place, Hippie Don said, "I can see that this is working, but I still think this guy could snap again and whack me." "You are right, Grasshopper," said Brickyard Don. "He might. But it is not in our interest for you to be clogging up your deeply philosophical mind with survival issues. You just concentrate on the larger social, political, and economic realities that have caused this poor man to be living out here on the streets instead of in a program where someone could be helping him and making sure that he is taking his medication. And let me be the bodyguard."

My Unique Heritage

My father is Irish. My mother is Greek. In the era prior to my enlightenment I often described myself as being descended from drunks and philosophers. However, the patient sensitivity training that I have received over the years through my association with the Unitarian Universalist community eventually showed me how hurtful it was for a person in my obvious position of influence (unknown folk-singer/author still holding a day job) to give credence to the myth that all Greeks are drunks and all Irish persons are descended from Socrates.

Transposed stereotypes aside, it is true that this unholy cross-pollination of cultures that courses mischievously through my veins has endowed me with a unique view of the world.

My parents were raised in a city that had a large Irish community and a large Greek community. The children of both groups of immigrants attended the same public schools. They played together on the same sports teams.

Eventually, they grew up and worked side by side in the local factories. But, as far as I can ascertain, my parents were the only two people from these ethnic communities who intermarried.

Intermarriage was, for the most part, unthinkable to these people because it was the nineteen-fifties and the era of touchy-feely interdenominational tolerance was still several years away.

Those were the good old days when the leaders of each sect would unabashedly refer to the rest of the world as heathens. They would predict, with certitude, the inevitable fiery eternity that awaited the unenlightened for their deliberate misinterpretation of the Word. This was a time when the fragile minds of the country's youth were not unnecessarily burdened with the complexities and nuances that might be encountered by someone who was looking at the world through something as rare and dangerous as a free will. It was a simpler time. One only needed to know three things.

1. Us guys good.
2. Those guys bad.
3. Do what we tell you.

My admittedly limited research into this ancient time reveals a population that, with the exception of some jazz musicians and the Zen Lunatics of San Francisco, respected authority. They loved authority. They fully expected to acquire great big gobs of it when they reached their thirties and they looked forward to having their authority universally respected and obeyed.

Within this world, where the church, the government,

and virtually anyone who qualified as an adult could march you off willingly in the name of any cause they said was just, the fact that my parents succeeded in marrying each other has always impressed me.

They had to fight both of their churches *and* both of their families. My dad was able to delay the fight with his family by letting them think that my mother was Italian. I have often imagined his family discussing her at the dinner table. "Well, there's no getting around it, her skin *is* really dark, but at least she believes in the Pope." As it turned out, they were right about her skin, but they were wrong about the Pope thing. To her, he was just a nice old man with a silly hat.

Within my mother's family, her intention to marry outside the Church caused great pain and suffering. Her father was the sexton at the Greek Church. He practically lived in there. He was the guy who took care of the altar. One of his most important responsibilities was to make sure that the frankincense barrel was always filled to the brim. Every Sunday Father Mihos would dramatically reduce the amount of oxygen in the building by burning just enough of this ancient incense to keep the congregation in that specific semiconscious state that lies delicately between asphyxiation and being coherent enough to realize that the service was four hours long.

The church was a very important part of my grand-father's life. His daughter's marriage was a big punch in the nose to him. When he learned that she intended to get married in the Catholic Church, he lost his mind. He could not even begin to cope with the knowledge that his daughter was not going to heaven and that she was extending this eternal catastrophe to his future grandchildren by her decision to raise them as Catholics.

He didn't go to the wedding.

At the time, the Catholic Church did not want Catholics to marry outside the church. They looked on it as being akin to marrying another species. However, things were loosening up a bit in the fifties and it was allowed under certain conditions. My mother was required to sign an official document promising to raise her children as Catholics. If she did this, the priest would perform the wedding. However, she would not be allowed to stand at the altar. That was where God drew the line.

She signed the paper and the priest performed the ceremony in the parking lot near the trash compactor for the CYO.

That part isn't true. It is true, though, that they wouldn't let her stand at the altar. God had a mean streak back then.

My parents were like two Davids fighting multiple Goliaths. They were all alone against two unreasonable global religions and two equally unreasonable families. All they had in their arsenal was a slingshot and an attitude problem.

This is my heritage. I am directly descended from two people with an incurable case of "you can all go to hell." This has proven to be their greatest and most enduring gift to me. The irony here is that, after almost fifty years in this marriage, my mother (wise-ass that she is) takes a certain pleasure in acknowledging that the churches and the families were both right.

*****

On Christmas day we would visit both sides of the

family. The Greeks all lived in a three-story tenement with the grandparents on the first floor and the aunts and uncles on the second and third. As kids, we would spend the day running up and down the stairs. Every door you opened revealed an apartment full of olive-skinned relatives who loved you. They loved you in a Mediterranean way. They fed you and they hugged you. Greeks hug. They pinch you on the cheek. They force food on you until you are ill and they squeeze you until you are gasping for air. Another noteworthy thing about these people is that there are precious few situations imaginable to them where being loud would be considered inappropriate.

We would leave there in the late afternoon and spend the rest of the day with the Irish half of the family. It all seemed perfectly normal back then, but in retrospect, it was like going to another planet.

The first obvious difference we encountered at the Irish house: no touching. Do not touch Irish people unless you are punching them. When we would arrive, my aunts and uncles would begrudgingly give us what I like to call the Irish Hug. An Irish Hug is when they put their arms around you as if they are being forced to do so at gunpoint. One quarter of one second into this reluctant embrace, they begin to tap you on the back. Back tapping is the key ingredient of the Irish hug. It is actually a message being tapped out in Morse code. This is the translation: "I hate this. Please let me go. I'll give you money. I need a drink."

The second obvious difference is that the Irish house provides safe harbor to an extremely sophisticated sense of humor. The complexities of the Irish sense of humor deserve an entire book of research. The Irish are born with a huge genetic advantage in the field of humor and storytelling. When an Irish person is weaving a tale, the listener is always engaged. The listener may actually be aware of the fact that what he or she is hearing is eighty percent blarney, but it is still captivating. This is a tremendous gift to the world. It also lends itself nicely to a career in politics.

It has always seemed to me that God overcompensated the Irish with immense wit and humor to make up for their abysmal ineptitude in cooking. If you are going to curse an entire nation to a lifetime of dinners boiled beyond recognition (my friend Katie says that an Irishwoman knows when her meat is done when it finally turns gray), you really do owe them something big in return.

The third obvious difference is volume. These are not loud people.

Several years ago I was installing an alarm system in a house full of Italians. The grandfather couldn't speak English. He used hand signals to beckon me over to a locked door at the back of the basement which opened to a room where he was making wine. We had a few glasses. It was very strong. After our second glass, we had miraculously bridged our language barrier. I pointed to the covering on a heat pipe. I said, "This is asbestos." He raised his glass and shouted, "Asbestos!" I raised my glass and shouted, "Asbestos, this will kill you!" He raised his glass and shouted, "Asbestos! Kill you!" and we had another drink.

Later that day I heard people yelling upstairs. The whole family was screaming at the top of their lungs. I was accustomed to hearing women yell. My mother yells all the time. My mother will yell about anything. It is one of her daily activities. Often she is not even angry. Her family just believes that the loudest person wins.

My dad, on the other hand, never yells when he gets angry. He seethes. As a child, my experience with the sound of a man raising his voice was that he had been seething over something for a week and this was the sound you heard when his head finally exploded. What always followed this sound was trouble—great big, very real trouble.

So, I am running wires over asbestos covered pipes in the Italian basement for an alarm system to protect the illegal winery when the entire family starts screaming. The men are so loud you could hear them a block away. I fully expect to hear gunfire. I consider climbing out a window, leaving my tools behind and trying to escape with my life. Instead, I climb to the top of the basement stairs, expecting to see blood and battered bodies. I peek around the door to the dining room and I see all ten of them sitting around the table passing around pastries. Passing around pastries and hollering at each other. For a moment it is all so surreal to me that I think the old man might have given me some psychedelic wine. (No wonder he needs an alarm system.) I watch for a while and finally realize that Italians are like Greeks, only louder. They can scream at you, feed you, call you an idiot, and love you, all at the same time. It is amazing to witness. It is SO not Irish.

A Much More
Deadly Strain

My kids make fun of me. They make fun of their mother too. There is nothing we can do about it. Many years ago we created these people through a mysterious biological process that bestowed upon them, among other things, our own unique wit and irreverence. Now in an impressive example of accelerated evolution they have taken this wit and irreverence to levels we never dreamed possible.

They'll be dancing in a group with their friends at a party and my son will suddenly yell out, "Everybody dance like Mom!" Instantly all the teenagers on the floor begin to perform their own individualized versions of the twirling hippie chick on acid at the Grateful Dead concert.

After they exhaust the creative possibilities of this delicious parental mockery, my daughter will yell, "Now everybody dance like Dad!" The entire group immediately breaks into improvisational interpretations of the mating dance of the adult male uncoordinated white guy who thinks he's cool. They call it the dork dance. This activity often culminates with them all lying in a heap on the floor and laughing uncontrollably.

In addition to having become a great source of comic relief for these young people, I have lost my ability to hold my own in repartee as well.

For instance my daughter recently told me that I needed a haircut. I replied that I had every intention of growing my hair down to my ass. She said that I was having a mid-life crisis. I told her that if I was having a mid-life crisis, *I* would have a new Corvette and *she* would have a new mommy.

Without missing a beat—before the last syllable of my sentence had traveled across the room to her ear—she said, "You can't afford that." Then she did the sassy daughter dance and sang:

> *You're having the p-o-o-o-r boy's*
> *Mid-life cri-i-i-i-sis.*
> *I think it's f-u-u-u-n-ny.*
> *Ha ha ha ha ha.*

She danced out the door laughing while I stood in the kitchen like Sonny Liston after the first round of his second fight with Cassius Clay. I was just looking around wondering what hit me and mumbling to myself that I used to be invincible.

There are many humbling moments in this business of child rearing. Perhaps the most impressive is when you realize that your own unique brand of obnoxious behavior has been processed and refined through the life experiences of your offspring only to reappear in the form of a much more deadly strain capable of conquering the world—beginning, of course, with you.

There is nothing in a person's life that says "it's time to pass the baton" more clearly than getting your big behind kicked by a younger, smarter, stronger, cuter version of yourself.

She Sings Me to Sleep with Laughter

I understand Exhaustion. Exhaustion and I have a long-standing and deeply intimate knowledge of one another. He knows how to slip into my life and make me miserable, and I know that he enjoys doing it. Over the past two decades I have carved out a small career as a singer-songwriter, while simultaneously maintaining a marriage, raising two children, and holding one, and sometimes two, day jobs. The currency with which I have paid for this music career is sleep. Exhaustion is the constant companion of all of us who choose to trade in this particular currency.

My daughter's bedroom is next to the bedroom where my wife, myself, and Exhaustion sleep. There has never been a real door on her room. We installed one of those flimsy folding doors that slide on tracks and open and close like an accordion. It has given her some privacy but has deprived her of one of the key ingredients of a complete adolescence—a door that slams. I must admit to several moments of glee over the years when the door-slamming exclamation point at the end of a teenage melodrama was replaced by the sound of little squeaky wheels sliding over aluminum runners.

Allow me to elaborate.

When my daughter was seventeen she and her mother would fight like two wild animals. Although I had no reason to believe that they were not speaking English, I was never able to decipher a single word. To me it sounded like someone had turned the Nature Channel up loud on the TV.

The dog and I would cower on the couch in the other room while these two women banshee-shrieked back and forth, the volume of their exchange increasing with each turn until an explosive cacophony was reached. That was often followed by the sound of them each stomping off to opposite ends of the house, leaving my dog and I awash in the angry estro-silence that I had come to know so well in those days.

In time, each would come to me separately.

First my daughter would complain about the injustices that had been imposed upon her by this woman that I had had the unforgivable lack of foresight to marry—the implication being that if during our courtship I could have envisioned the sadistic pleasure that my future bride would eventually derive from consistently denying basic human freedoms to her children, I would certainly have chosen more carefully.

Since my lack of credentials as a visionary were obvious and abundant to my daughter, she would fire only a cursory volley across the bow of my abysmal decisionmaking and then move swiftly to the matter at hand—the matter of justice, how it had been stolen from her and how she expected me to snatch it from the jaws of her oppressor and return it to its rightful home.

The fact that this otherwise observant young woman was suffering under the delusion that her father was somehow capable of extracting justice from her mother betrayed a fundamental lack of understanding regarding the hierarchy of our family.

The truth (which I had not the heart to tell her) is that if I were capable of getting justice from that woman, I would get some for myself.

Although I knew that I could do nothing to affect the oppression under which she suffered, I felt an obligation to pretend otherwise. Taking my cue from the dog, I listened attentively with a look of empathy and unconditional love on my face as my daughter described, with righteous indignation, the many tethers that had been fastened upon her liberty by my evil dictator spouse.

And much like the dog, I could only comprehend a fraction of her words. That's because I have an attention deficit problem . . . especially when I don't like what people are saying to me.

I could see her lips moving but it sounded very similar to the way that the teachers talk in Charlie Brown cartoons: "Waaah wah wah waah wah wah MY MOTHER!!! Waah wah wah waah."

Eventually realizing my utter ineffectiveness in all matters Mom, my daughter would depart. Her departure would be followed shortly by her mother's arrival. "Waah wah wah waah wah wah YOUR DAUGHTER!!! Waah wah wah waah."

In the subsequent second icy estro-silence I would marvel at the realization that if I closed my eyes when my wife and daughter were complaining to me, I couldn't tell which one was talking.

It has, I must confess, occurred to me that the problem these two people have with each other might have something to do with the fact that they are identical.

It's just a theory.

One of the more memorable of these episodes took place in my daughter's seventeenth year. Following some indecipherable banshee-shrieking, she stepped back and defied her captors. "I'm seventeen years old and you CAN'T tell me what to do! I'll come home at twelve o'clock or one o'clock or any time I feel like it! And pretty soon I'll be eighteen and then I'll be able to do whatever I want!"

Then she did an abrupt about-face, accepting no further rebuttals, and stomped up the stairs. Beside her little accordion door she turned and hollered some more.

Her mother and I stood in the living room in wild-eyed amazement at the animal noises being launched from the second story of our domicile. Our daughter's voice at full volume rolled down the stairwell and washed over us like an adolescent tsunami.

"AND WHEN I TURN EIGHTEEN I AM MOVING OUT OF THIS HOUSE!!!"

One second later her proclamation was followed by the sound of her attempting to slam her accordion door.

Weekee weekee weekee . . . click.

After laughing so hard we could barely breathe, I eventually regained enough composure to stand at the foot of the stairs and call, "Let me make sure I understand this correctly. You're gonna leave home when you're eighteen weekee weekee weekee." My wife and I were then again immediately overcome with giant swells of laughter.

Parents of teenagers can expect very few victories. However, if you remove your teenager's slammable door and replace it with a little weekee weekee accordion door, your friend Don promises you occasional moments of absolute joy.

OK, let's get back to the story I really wanted to tell.

One night when my daughter was fifteen, Exhaustion was beating me about the head and shoulders. It was 11:30 P.M. I could hear the 6 A.M. setting on the alarm clock actually taunting me. "I'm going to ring as soon as you close your eyes big guy."

My daughter was on the phone with one of her girlfriends. She was laughing. It was the kind of laugh that can only come from a fifteen-year-old girl.

As something of a comedian, I have spent a disproportionate amount of my life studying the different sounds of laughter. In addition to the obvious fact that each person has his or her own unique laugh (it's kind of like a fingerprint when you think about it), there are several different *types* of laughter. The "I can't believe it, that's just like my mother" warm laugh. The "Oh my God, did he really just say that" shock laugh. The polite, unenthusiastic, almost obligatory, laugh. The "this guy is really scary" nervous laugh. And the awkward, uncomfortable laughter that comes from mean-spirited, victim-oriented humor.

To the untrained ear, all of these may sound pretty much the same. However, the laughter of a fifteen-year-old girl on the telephone with her best friend is a sound unlike any other on earth.

I am lying in bed. I am so tired I could cry. I am not only being taunted by Exhaustion and my alarm clock, but also by all the realities inflicted upon my life by every poor decision I have ever made. Sleep, even just a little bit of it, is the only remedy. Unfortunately, I am being denied this cure by the shrieks and wails of hysterical teenage laughter devilishly dancing out of my daughter's room.

I resolve that I must address the situation. I then begin the process of deciding which of my two available Dad identities I should manifest in the bedroom doorway of my inconsiderate daughter—the goal being to deliver unto her the Dad persona that will bring blessed quiet back to my domicile as quickly as possible with the least amount of energy output and ramifications.

The first Dad incarnation that comes to mind is the stereotypical blusterer. This is the one in which I storm over to her room and, with all the self-righteous indignation available to Dad Number One, I identify her crimes against humanity and the reasons why they are personally offensive to me. Then, using the loud, severely agitated and totally unreasonable Dad Number One voice I say, "I'm trying to get some sleep here! You don't care that I have to get up at six in the morning. Why should you? You get to sleep till noon. All you ever think about is yourself. It would never even occur to you that other people might actually be living in this house!" Then I flex my dictatorial muscle by saying, "Hang that phone up right now."

And then there is quiet.

Quiet anger.

Quiet resentment.

And quiet plotting of revenge.

You see, Dad Number One always gets much more quiet than he bargained for. That's because he is one hundred percent bluster and zero percent circumspection. His shortsightedness is legendary. The method by which he seeks to attain his immediate goal actually fortifies the resolve of the opposition. He wins the battle at the expense of the war. He is a pawn of Exhaustion and is destined to spend his waking hours in an endless cycle of explosive bravado followed by the need to apologize for it.

Once Dad Number One is finished blowing off steam and asserting his authority in my mind, he gives the podium to Dad Number Two. This dad is also driven to action by Exhaustion but, unlike his surly cousin, he lacks the will to fight. Instead, he is a pleader. His method is to crawl out of bed looking as pitiful as possible and to speak in a defeated monotone. "Ariel honey, I have to get up early. Could you please use the phone downstairs?" Although sad and emasculated, this Dad, if he accomplishes his goal, usually does so without creating a situation that he will feel obligated to repair later.

On this occasion I choose to manifest Dad Number Two. I conjure up my defeated monotone and roll it around in my mouth. I am preparing to climb out of bed and address the situation when a hitherto unknown door in my mind opens up and out steps Dad Number Three. He speaks. "Dad Number One is an asshole and Dad Number Two is an idiot. The problem here is not with the sounds in this house, it is with the way you are choosing to hear them." I think, "Great, Dad Number Three is a fucking philosopher." I say, "Is this going to take long? I really need to get some sleep." He tells me to shut up. Then he says, "Let's take a look at what we actually have here. You are about to take action that will curtail the sounds of laughter in your home. Is this really what you want? Would you prefer your home to be filled with the sounds of anger or crying? The sounds that fill a home are part and parcel of the memories that are created there. *Quiet* is what happens in a home when you are alone in it. Be careful how much of this you wish for." Then he says it again. "The problem here is not with the sounds in this house, it is with the way you are choosing to hear them."

And then I get it. I don't just get it a little bit. I really get it. I completely get it. I get it in the center of my solar plexus. I grok it. It must be like this when suddenly one day you understand jazz. I say to myself, "What kind of a father can't go to sleep to the sound of his daughter laughing?"

Instantly, as if the asking of the question initiated the metamorphosis, all the sounds emerging from my daughter's room are transformed. They become music. They become summer rain. I lie back and let them wash over me. All the pores in my body open up and absorb them. I drink in the miracle of my daughter's teenage laughter. It is magic. It is giddy. It is a sound so complete that it seems as if every one of her molecules is laughing. There is no distinction between my daughter the young adult and laughter itself. It is one glorious symphony, light and lovely. She sings me to sleep with laughter. I dream of woodwinds and of small birds dancing gracefully upon delicate breaths of wind. In the morning I awake refreshed. Exhaustion is gone and will not return until the day has wrestled from me my zest.

There is a distinct lightness in the early morning quiet of my home. I glance in upon the sleeping figure of my daughter, beautiful and at peace. I whistle a line from "The Dance of the Sugarplum Fairies" and begin my day.

The Adventures of Alarm Man

Chapter One

Alarm Man hates rich people. They give him heartburn.

That's not always true. Sometimes they give him acid indigestion, ulcers, or exploding hemorrhoids. In fact, I named one of my hemmies after one of my most insufferable rich customers. I call it Sarah Schwartz.

"I can't sit on this wooden chair any more, my Sarah Schwartz is killing me."

Mrs. Schwartz had a house in Chestnut Hill. She called it a house. It was really a castle.

Chestnut Hill is Alarm Man Hell. It's where the richest people in the state live. No houses in this neighborhood are worth less than five million dollars. And, oh yeah, no matter what your street map says, it is *not* in Brookline and it is *not* in Newton. Chestnut Hill is an island, an entire universe unto itself.

When I pulled into the driveway to work on the alarm, I was thinking about the last time that I was in this house. It was several years ago. I had been having one of those days where everything that I touched turned to shit. Somehow I had been transformed from a qualified licensed alarm technician into the good fairy's incompetent stepbrother. Earlier that same day I had waved my magic wand, with the best of intentions, at a perfectly functional five-thousand-dollar alarm system and it was instantly changed into a sputtering, blinking, useless, pile o' shit. (It did occur to me that it might be time to recalibrate my magic wand.)

I noticed that the name of my favorite hemorrhoid was not on the work order. She had apparently sold her castle to some other fuckhead after whom (it seemed likely) I would be naming my next disgusting medical problem.

The new owner's name was Sloan. As I rang the doorbell, I was thinking how nice a name that would be for a kidney stone.

A carpenter answered the door. The new owners were gutting the castle and building an addition. Several of the existing alarm wires had been damaged, destroyed, or buried behind new walls and ceilings during the construction. I was to repair and/or excavate the old wires and run new ones to the addition. In other words, this was a nightmare, or—to put it in the understated terminology of the alarm man—a fucking abortion.

The new owners weren't home. I wandered through the house shaking my head and mumbling proletarian obscenities. This was a three-story, twenty-room house with a four-foot thick granite foundation. There were brick and mortar fire stops in every wall and no pipe drop from the attic. It was the kind of house that rich people build with the specific intention of infuriating Alarm Man.

No one besides electricians and alarm installers gives a flying fuck about what it takes to run wires in a house like this. So I never get to rant about it to anyone outside the business. This is extremely unsatisfying because anyone who *is* in the business, while nodding their heads and pretending to listen, is really just waiting for you to stop talking so they can tell you about their own even more unbelievable wire-running nightmare. This type of extremely annoying one-upmanship permeates all inter-alarm guy conversation.

However, as if the stories to this point in this collection weren't punishment enough for buying this book, I am going to take further advantage of your generous nature by using this time to describe exactly what it takes to get a wire from the control panel in Mrs. Kidneysloan's colossal basement to the window behind the grand piano in her Great Room.

In a normal house—you know, one with only, say, twelve rooms—Alarm Man would drill a three-quarter-inch hole beneath the window and then either drill down to the basement with a long bit or drill up into the wall cavity from the basement. He would then use his catch snake to fish out the wire.

But your run-of-the-mill five-million-dollar, twenty-room Chestnut Hill castle is guaranteed to have a massive stone foundation. So if by some miracle Alarm Man *can* drill past the brick and mortar fire stop and into the basement beneath the window, his drill bit will still be three feet away from the inside basement wall. And of course he can't just reach up there and grab it, because the ceiling is always made of plaster and wire mesh.

It can take four hours to wire one window. By the

time it is done, there is a big hole in the basement ceiling, our hero is covered with the kind of old ceiling plaster that looks suspiciously like asbestos, his hands and arms are gashed open from jagged wire mesh, the boss wants to know why it is taking so long, and Mrs. Kidneysloan is looking at her basement ceiling and suggesting that the company should buy her a new house.

Alarm Man hates rich people.

I was sitting on the front steps, contemplating whether to call out sick for the next two weeks or to just quit altogether, when a brand new black BMW pulled into the driveway. "This has to be the owner," I thought. I pulled my face out of my hands, suppressed my contempt, manufactured a professional veneer, and walked over to introduce myself.

The woman who arose slowly from the front seat was tall and thin, perhaps in her early forties. She made direct eye contact with me and flashed me a smile. It seemed genuine and it had more than a hint of "happy to see you" in it. It was the last thing I expected and it threw my whole game off balance.

Chestnut Hill had been part of my work area for ten years. I had installed or repaired alarms in dozens of homes in that neighborhood. I would occasionally be caught off guard by the magnitude of the job or by the ineptitude of the person who sold it. But I was *never* surprised by what happened when I met the customer.

It had always been the same.

I would ring the doorbell. The owner would open the door. I would be given a quick head-to-toe assessment, followed by a facial expression that very clearly said, "I know I have to let you in here to do this work, but please don't sit on my furniture." Then two things would invariably occur. *They* would conceal that face with one that feigned less arrogance, and *I* would resist the temptation to tell them that I could read their mind and that they could rest easy because if I had to take a shit during the day, I would go down to McDonald's to do so.

I had approached the BMW with all my emotional defenses in a heightened state. I was prepared to absorb her initial snobbery, play my predetermined role in the Brahmin and Untouchable game, and then move forward to the job at hand like a professional.

As I was introducing myself, she was gathering up a bag full of breakfast sandwiches and half a dozen cups of coffee from the back seat. She apologized for not picking up anything for me but she had forgotten that I was coming.

I followed her to the addition at the rear of the house. We walked up a long 2 x 10 plank that sloped down from the threshold in lieu of a stairway to be built later and then we proceeded into the open doorway. Inside, five carpenters were framing walls, cutting wood on a table saw, and banging nails. A glow came over them when they saw her. They shut off the saw and put down their tools. They all gathered around a makeshift workbench where she dispensed breakfast and engaged them in conversation.

I worked on her alarm system for five days. It was dirty and dusty. It sucked. It was hell. I hated it.

Each day at noon Mrs. Sloan would appear with coffee and sandwiches. All work would stop. She knew everyone by name. She looked you in the eye when she talked and she seemed genuinely concerned about everyone.

Alarm Man was skeptical.

Why would someone so outrageously wealthy (my whole

house would fit in her living room) care about the day-to-day challenges of a bunch of nail bangers and wire jockeys?

It had to be a scam.

Maybe she was a brilliant businesswoman who had learned that you can get your help to do a much better job if you can fool them into thinking that you give two shits about them.

On Monday and Tuesday I studied her closely looking for a telltale glimpse of contrived empathy. I saw nothing. By Wednesday I had concluded that she was either the best actress I had ever seen or she was the most endangered species of bird on earth—a genuinely compassionate multi-millionaire.

I could hear David Attenborough's British accent in my mind. "For one hundred and twenty years it was believed that the yellow-breasted compassionate millionaire was extinct. Then in 1995 an alarm man, working in the highest regions of Chestnut Hill, happened upon the world's only known surviving female."

By noon on Thursday I was just another charmed workman gathering around her for coffee and conversation.

Chapter Two

On Friday evening I was sitting in my office. I call it an office. It's just a little room with a computer in it and bunch of papers and other assorted crap piled up all over the place.

The phone rang. I picked up the receiver and said, "Hello." After a few seconds a voice said, "Hi Don, this is Jeff Fowler here." A blast of fear shot through me. My hands started to shake and my stomach became simultaneously tight and woozy. I took a moment to gather myself and to make sure that my voice wouldn't reveal my anxiety. I said, "Hi Jeff. How are you?" I didn't do a very good job with the concealing-the-emotions thing because my voice cracked and my trepidation splashed out all over the phone.

It didn't seem to matter.

Jeff Fowler was speaking to me from a distant place. It's not really a listening place. It's that terrible zone that lies between what you've known, loved, built, and lived for, and complete, unstoppable change.

The fear that was causing my hands to shake was initiated by some ancient molecular part of me that recognized, by the sad, dreamy, distance in his voice, that he was calling me from the place that all fathers and husbands fear and dread. We fear it and we dread it because we are born with the knowledge that some day we may be on the initiating end of this situation.

"It's been a long hard struggle for Ruthie. It's pretty much over now. We're stopping treatments and we're going to let her go."

The sentence came out of my telephone and hung in the air before me. It was as if I needed to actually see those last six words, that simply hearing them wasn't enough.

Two years earlier, on a New England summer day so perfect that it seemed fictional, I was at a cookout in the country with lots of music and laughter. Ruthie was in remission. She looked great. The sun simply adored her this day. It lit her in a way that intentionally drew your eye to how alive she was as she sat on the front porch of the old house with all her friends and held court.

She was explaining her theory about the many unappreciated benefits of having an incarcerated husband to a group of younger women, benefits like "conjugal visits when *you* feel like it, and the joy of being able to leave him in a cage afterwards." She was bursting with a rare combination of wit, irreverence, love and laughter. It made her seem like the poster child for the life force.

Later, with Jeff sitting beside her, they told the story of how he first realized that he might have a drinking problem. They told it in the style of a married couple with great timing, each telling a section and then letting the other pick up and carry the story forward.

Jeff: I would be out drinking at night. I'd come home drunk and climb into bed. One morning, I wake up and I'm soaking wet from the waist down. Oh my God! I didn't think I was so drunk that I would piss myself. The next night, it's the same thing.

Ruthie: I'm, like, I told you that you had a problem. You need to get help. This is out of control. I cannot live like this.

Jeff: And every night it's the same thing. If I get hammered or if I just have a few beers after work, I wake up soaked. I knew I drank too much, but now I'm thinking that I'm a lot further gone than I thought. For Christ sakes, Louie the Loser, who drinks a fifth of Wild Irish Rose for breakfast, probably only pisses his pants once a week.

Ruthie: And I'm disgusted. I want to help and everything, but this is grossing me out.

Jeff: I find out where the local AA meetings are and I decide to start going.

Ruthie: So, I'm changing the bed one day. I throw the sheets and blankets on the floor and I lean on the mattress with one hand and reach across to grab a pillow, and a small stream of water shoots up into the air from Jeff's side of the bed.

Jeff: It never occurred to either of us that if you wake up wet every morning it might be from a hole in your waterbed.

Ruthie: Now I'm thinking to myself, 'He's still a drunk and a pain in the ass, and now he's going to AA. How exactly does it benefit me to tell him about this?'

Jeff: You did tell me though.

Ruthie: Yeah, but I never told you that I actually poked the hole in the mattress on purpose.

The sun was sinking. They sat beside each other, each occasionally resting a hand upon the other's shoulder as they talked. It was an oasis of real joyful living placed gently—perfectly—between months of unknowable suffering.

Alarm Man hates breast cancer.

Jeff talked to me for perhaps ten minutes on the phone that evening. I listened. It wasn't the kind of listening that one normally does, where you hear the words, process the meaning, and respond. I was listening from the part of me that was born knowing that I may have to make this phone call myself some day. The only words I actually heard, the only ones I really remember, were the ones that he repeated several times to me.

"Be sure to hug that beautiful wife of yours."

"I will Jeff."

Chapter Three

I sat in the chair with the phone in my hand and stared at the wall. Jeff had hung up. It was too much to process right away. I could hear laughter rising up from the living room. My son and daughter were down there with their mom.

She has a great laugh, my wife. It's these short, high-pitch, staccato half-yelps. It always sounds beautiful to me, but there is a particularly magnificent texture to it when she is laughing with her children. It's a warmer, fuller sound. It says, "This is the happiest I can ever be." When I hear it, I get younger. If I could hear my wife laugh with her children every day, I'd never grow old.

The telephone in my hand suddenly began to yak. It was that dreadful "I'm off the hook and I demand to be hung up immediately" sound. It dragged me out of my reverent analysis of the sounds of laughter. I obediently did as my telephone commanded and then I went to bed.

Chapter Four

On Sunday night I got an email from a friend that Ruthie had died.

At 8:00 Monday morning I was with Mrs. Sloan in her kitchen. I was there to drop off some blueprints and to get her to sign off on the work I had done the week before. I had just finished showing her how to use her alarm system when I was overcome by a massive swell of emotion. It was a tidal wave. It was as if my mind had spent the weekend studying the information it had received without including me in the process, and then, at 8:15 on Monday, it broke the news to me. "Your friend is dead."

After signing the completion form, Mrs. Sloan looked up and asked me what was wrong. I should have said,

"Nothing," and left, but I couldn't stop myself. I said, "A friend of mine died from breast cancer yesterday and it just hit me. I'm sorry. I just need a minute to pull it together here." But I didn't pull myself together. I just kept talking. "What's killing me today is not so much that she's gone but that I'm not going to get to tell her what a great gal she is and how knowing her has made my life better. It only takes a minute to say these things, but there are no more minutes for her and me."

Alarm Man was losing it.

I was looking at the floor. Without looking up, I said, "This is how easy it is. I've worked in this neighborhood for ten years. I've met a lot of people up here. Some were nice. Some were not. But I've never met anyone like you before. You are absolutely amazing to me. The way you treat everyone with respect and compassion. The way you are genuinely interested in the lives of these people who are working in your house. The way your generosity seems to roll off you naturally and gracefully. I love the way you walk in the world. It has made a deep impression on me and I just wanted to take this minute to tell you so."

As I was speaking the last of these words, I was coming back to reality from beneath my emotional tidal wave and I was realizing that I had taken a gigantic leap over the alarm guy/customer boundary. I was sure that when I looked up, I would see the face of a woman who felt that she was in the presence of an unbalanced and potentially dangerous individual. I began to picture a closed-door meeting with my supervisor with me trying to answer the question, "What the hell did you say to her that made her call the cops?"

With the trepidation of a person who knows his

situation is irreparable, I forced myself to look up at her. To my astonishment she wasn't dialing 911 or pressing the panic button on her new alarm system.

She was crying.

"How much more surreal can this situation possibly become?" I thought. She wiped her eyes with the heel of her palm and said, "Don't get me wrong, I didn't grow up poor. My parents had money. I owned my own business, a flower store. My favorite part of the business was getting to know the customers. I have always been genuinely interested in people and their lives. I never understood why people look down on other people. And in the circles that my husband and I are in these days, there is just so much of it. It always upsets me. Thank you for taking the time to say what you said to me. No one has ever done that before. I'm really sorry to hear about your friend."

We then had an awkward moment where we turned back into alarm man and rich lady. Silently we agreed to keep the memory of our undefended humanity to ourselves. I gathered up my paperwork and left.

From there I went to the office to pick up some equipment for my afternoon job. During my time with Mrs. Sloan I had been out of my mind. I was drunk on emotion and not completely aware of what I was saying. When I got to the office it was more like I had a little buzz on—an afterglow. I was experiencing a mild euphoria.

I was thinking about how easy it was to tell Mrs. Sloan how extraordinary she was and how wonderful that had made her feel. "If it's this damn easy, how come I don't do more of it? What exactly is the down side?" I opened the door to the office area and stood there for a moment and took a good long look at the place.

It was exactly what you would expect. A big square room with windows that don't open. They don't build office buildings with windows that can open any more. That's because when office workers have the ability to open the windows, it's only a matter of time before they begin hurling themselves out of them.

I began to see the room as being divided into cubicle neighborhoods.

The ghetto, where the data entry and less significant sales persons reside, is like a Jamaican shantytown. The cubicle walls are only four feet high. If you are a data entry person working in shantytown, the pasty, bulbous craniums of virtually any person of average height in the company can appear above any of your three cubicle walls at any moment of any day.

It's like working in a bad circus dream.

One of the benefits of living in the suburban middle-class neighborhood of the office is that your cubicle walls are six feet high. Don't get me wrong, you still only get three of them, but all the big nightmarish clown heads of the office can't just pop up around you, like balloons on strings, whenever they feel like it.

The posh neighborhood (the Chestnut Hill of the workplace) is not made up of cubicles. These people have actual offices that feature the greatest perk in the entire hierarchy of middle management—the door.

I walked into the ghetto. I sat down with a saleswoman named Donna with whom I had worked for the past year. After a few how-are-yous I said, "I just love working with you. You're always so nice to me. I love the way you genuinely care about your customers and how you never oversell them or scare them into buying more than they need. It makes me think that eventually the real salespeople are going to find out that you are incurably honest and revoke your membership to the 'fuck your customers' club."

Freakish balloon heads began to pop up and peer down quizzically upon us from above her ghetto walls.

"I also really love the way your face lights up when you talk about your son. You're amazing, and it's a pleasure to know you."

All this took less than two minutes.

Chapter Five

On Saturday of the next weekend, as I was writing this story, my wife was preparing dinner downstairs in the kitchen. I had just completed Chapter Three when I heard a lot of pounding. I thought she might be tenderizing some meat. This is a very entertaining enterprise that I have seen her do before, where she takes a silver mallet with rough edges and beats the shit out of a helpless piece of chicken. It's hysterical. The pounding continued for what seemed like a long time. I began to think that this was either a particularly tough piece of fowl or that my wife was using the tenderizing of our dinner to take out some frustrations that might have accrued during the week.

However, both these theories were debunked by the sound of her voice calling to me from the back yard.

"Don, open the door!"

She had locked herself out of the house.

I went down and let her in. She began to nag at me. "Didn't you hear me pounding on the door?" She has a great nag, my wife. It's this condescending tone, delivered with an indignant head tilt and a facial expression that calls me an imbecile. It always infuriates me. It accelerates my aging process. If I could hear my wife talk to me like I am an idiot every day, I'd be dead in a year.

I went back upstairs and thought about my friends Jeff and Ruthie.

"Be sure to hug that beautiful wife of yours."

"I will, Jeff."

Not right this minute, but I will.

Five Minutes
at my Friend's Wedding

You'll be pleased to know I found scholarly support
for your thesis about disco music. The respected cultural
theorist Richard Dyer wrote (1979) that disco's emphasis
on "open-ended, mutating polyrhythm and timbre restores
eroticism to the whole body," and contrasts radically with
the "indelibly phallo-centric music" of rock.

Terence Hegarty
(personal communication with Don White)

Preface

Several people have told me that my daughter is a very
good writer. I have never seen any of her work, but the
circumstantial evidence is impressive. A few months ago I
told her the general idea that I had for this story and I

asked her if she would help me by writing a few paragraphs that I could include as a preface. I thought that it might lay an objective foundation for the tale I hoped to tell.

She said she would do it.

She was humoring me.

I asked her about it again yesterday.

"Yo, best daughter, how's that story coming?"

"Yo, best father, not so good. You do know why I haven't written that piece for you, right?"

"Yes daughter, it's because you don't love me."

"Yes father, that's true, but besides that?"

"Hmm . . . Is it because you're on the crack and that's consuming all of your free time?"

"Well yes, of course, but that's not the only reason."

"Well then, why don't you be a nice daughter and tell your poor old dopey dad what that other reason is."

"It's because you are 'Daddy Don the Writer,' and I am way too intimidated to show you my work."

"You are aware, best daughter, that there is a lot of evidence to support the claim that I don't know the first thing about writing."

"Yes, Daddy I am, but for some reason that hasn't made it any easier to show you my stories. Love ya. Gotta go."

Then she bounced down the stairs and disappeared into the night.

I had hoped to begin this story with a first hand account of that time in a young girl's life when first love has her up all night on the phone talking with her girlfriend.

Despite the fact that the shadow that Daddy Don casts over the other writers in his family is imaginary and has been manufactured by disregarding all the available evidence, (I'm not even sure if that comma belongs before these parentheses), I am now left to muddle my way through a subject about which I could not possibly know less.

I did attempt to glean some insight into this matter from the other woman in my life.

Here is the conversation I had with my wife this morning.

"What do you remember about being all giddy on the phone with your girlfriends over your first kiss, first dance or prom night that might help me with this story I'm writing?"

"I don't have any memories like that. I was a tomboy. Giddy girls were weird to me. I didn't get it. Sure I went to the dances, but I was from the projects so I wasn't in the cliques with those girls. We danced. We didn't gab on the phone. Plus, even if I wanted to, my dad wouldn't let us. If you were on the phone for more than two minutes, he would start yelling about his message units. What is a message unit anyway? I've been paying phone bills for thirty years, and I still don't know what the hell he was talking about. In my house you used the phone to make plans. 'Meet you down the park in an hour, bye.' I had three brothers, no phone privileges and frankly I was way too cool to be giddy."

So, because one woman in my life was too cool to know anything about the first love giddies and the other one exaggerates my talents as an excuse to avoid helping me, my options regarding the job at hand are severely limited. I could, I suppose, just pretend that, by virtue of my sensitivity and acute observational skills, I can see into the hearts and minds of women and am therefore qualified to lecture on all their dazzling emotional complexities.

Right.

I was born to and raised by a woman. That same woman also gave birth to a female human with whom I shared a home until I was seventeen. At twenty-two I married a woman and have now spent more than half my life with her. I also played an admittedly small but enjoyable role in the creation of another female whom I have since helped raise to adulthood.

Despite a lifetime of intimacy with these creatures, I am no less mystified by them today than I was in my childhood.

My bewilderment does not arise from an inability to recognize what is going on with them. As a matter of survival, I have learned to quickly identify and respond to a vast array of inherently female unexplained emotional phenomena.

However, being able to recognize a particular emotional moment and behaving in a way that minimizes its natural tendency toward—oh, shall we say, for the sake of argument, unreasonableness—is not the same as understanding *why* it is happening.

For example, I know the "don't touch me—don't go out" monster when I see it, but that doesn't mean that I understand what great purpose is served by its appearance in my home every twenty-eight days.

Think of me as a mouse in a laboratory. There are two identical tubes that feed my cage. The first one delivers a tasty treat to me. The second one gives me an electric shock. As a rodent with a limited capacity for analysis, I have no idea why a feeding tube that looks exactly like the one that delivers me something delicious would deliberately choose to give me a painful jolt.

I only know I shouldn't touch it.

If I were to apply my profound lack of understanding

on this subject to pen and paper, I suspect the end result would be akin to a story about what it's like to be a virtuoso pianist written by a man who had once photographed a virtuoso pianist.

So, since I am clearly unqualified for the job, I thought perhaps I could get you to do it for me. I'll just tell you what I'm looking for, and you can reach back into your old love memories and dredge up the appropriate recollections and associated feelings. When events in the story provoke a reference back to first love, feel free to call upon your own unique memory.

It'll be interactive.

You will contribute significantly to the writing of this story. And in accordance with applicable laws you will receive absolutely no compensation.

Welcome to the big league world of publishing.

Let's try it and see what happens.

For those women who, like Mrs. White, are too cool to be giddy, it's important to know that the feelings we are concerned with here aren't the exclusive domain of rich suburban white girls with braces and a bedroom wall covered with boy band posters.

I am operating under the assumption that the hormone explosion that takes place in the metabolism of the cheerleader when the captain of the football team asks her to the prom is identical to the one that occurs inside the girl with the green hair and multiple piercings when she gets dragged into the mosh pit by the greasy-haired bass player of her favorite alternative band.

It is the actual emotions and the place that the memories of first love occupy in the fabric of a woman as she matures that is relevant to this story, not whether she is cool or not.

OK, ladies first.

This shouldn't take long. All you need to do is to unlock the memory of your first love. Don't let yourself be distracted by how he turned out. Giving any thought to his receding hairline, his beer belly, or his current terms of incarceration will prove counterproductive. Just picture him back then when he was the boy of your dreams.

Now conjure up whatever qualifies in your mind as the moment with dreamy boy that released your "first love" hormones. Was it a kiss, a slow dance, a walk on the beach? Once you've snagged the memory, just dive all the way back in.

Remember the way you felt and allow yourself to feel that way again. Picture yourself going home afterwards. Who was the one person you just absolutely had to tell about it? Remember how the excitement of reliving it with your girlfriend was almost as delicious as the moment itself. Allow yourself to feel the first love bounce in your step as you walked to meet him the next time.

OK, now the men.

Don't be scared. I'm not expecting you to do anything unreasonable like evolve into a sensitive, compassionate life form. I think that this is going to be a pretty good story, but we can all agree that no composition of mine is going to do in an hour what evolution has failed to accomplish in thousands of years. However, I am confident that you can complete the task at hand and still remain the one-celled organism that we have all grown to know and love.

You will also be relieved to know that in order to participate in this interactive composition it is not necessary for you to travel to a land as distant and mysterious as the one that exists inside the head of a woman in love.

The first thing we need to do is to acknowledge the distinction between the romantic memories that women have when they think of first love and the disgusting ones that you have.

I am not going to spend any time here listing the many obvious fundamental differences between men and women. *That* is what standup comedy is for. (Standup, for those of you who are interested in such things, is also an excellent place to acquire formulaic oversimplifications on the differences between New Yorkers and Californians and between Caucasians and African Americans.)

Let's take a look inside your head. As you can see, most of the big rooms are dedicated to sex. But way over there in the corner is a small door leading to a tiny control panel that is dedicated to protecting the women that (most of) you are programmed *not* to have sex with.

It's the sister/daughter room.

Very few heterosexual men are ever going to be able to understand the language that is spoken in woman-in-love land, but from the sister/daughter room you get a view that is unencumbered by your genetic responsibility to perpetuate the species. This is where you go to write your preface.

Think sister or daughter. Think prom night. Look at her. Could she be any more beautiful? Don't let your mind get bogged down with trying to figure out why this means so much to her. Just look at her face. It is telling you that she couldn't be happier or more excited. If the night lives up to her expectations, she will treasure it all the way to the nursing home.

Her face, that dress, the glow that hangs in the room after she closes the door—they all communicate the immense importance of this night in a way that you are perfectly capable of comprehending if you view it from the father/ brother section of the sister/daughter room.

Chapter One
The Neighborhood Bar

Kenny's was a neighborhood bar located on the corner of Nelson Street and Western Avenue in Lynn, Massachusetts. Not unlike most of the other corner bars of the time, there had not been a tremendous amount of thought or expense committed to the décor. Kenny's was going for that early sixties, no-frills, "if-that's-my-wife-tell-her-I-just-left" dive bar feel.

It did so beautifully.

There was a row of barstools, a creaky wooden floor, two small wobbly tables, a centrally located cigarette vending machine and two occasionally working toilets.

This establishment featured a conspicuous absence of such amenities as food, fancy drinks, coherent conversation, and air conditioning. Within these walls the primary activity was alcohol consumption—alcohol consumption of the shot-and-beer-chaser variety.

If you stood on the sidewalk in front of the building and looked to your left and then to your right you would see seven other barrooms and two liquor stores.

It was as if this section of Western Avenue, from McDonough Square to Market Square, had been zoned by the city for the development and subsequent maintenance of the local alcoholic constituency.

In addition to their common disregard for interior decoration, bars like Kenny's are deliberately designed to keep out sunlight and the eyes of people passing by. They are windowless caverns. When you enter and the door closes behind you, you feel subterranean. In midsummer, however, the absence of windows and air conditioning sometimes forces the troglodyte patrons to leave the front door open.

And so it was on this July day in 1973 that the door to Kenny's Corner Bar was held open by a metal frame barstool with a torn red plastic seat.

Standing across the street in the sunlight and looking into this place, I felt like I had discovered a portal into a secret dark dimension, an underground alternate universe, or perhaps even the nether world itself.

Three shadowy figures huddled together at the end of the bar that was furthest from the toxic sunlight. As I watched, one of them turned toward the light and walked out into the West Lynn afternoon. It was like seeing a raccoon in the middle of the day.

He stood there for a moment with what can only be described as a crazed look in his eye (perhaps the result of a vitamin D deficiency). Then he picked up the barstool with one hand and threw it into the middle of the street, where it crashed against the front passenger door of a brown station wagon with a woman and three horrified children inside.

The rabid raccoon turned around, walked back into the bar, and, as the door closed behind him, he presumably sat down and ordered a shot and a beer.

Chapter Two
The Neighborhood Church

My Dad grew up on Wyman Street. His bedroom window looked out at Sacred Heart Catholic Church.

I am writing this in October of 2003. It has been a tough year for the Catholic Church, especially here in Boston. I guess you could call it the year of priests behaving badly, or more precisely, the year of priests being held accountable for years of behaving badly.

The local news programs have reported one scandal after another featuring pedophile priests, morally corrupt bishops, and ultimately the resignation in disgrace of Cardinal Law.

For the record, I want to state here that I have never been touched by a priest—physically, spiritually, or otherwise. I did once kiss a ring on the hand of Cardinal Cushing, but, despite what my lawyer says, I did not feel violated by the experience.

As a kid I went to church every Sunday. I received communion. I went to confession. I was confirmed. I even went to religious classes after school.

I met many priests, nuns, and Catholic teachers. They were all nice people. I do not have a story to tell of how someone in a position of power in the church robbed me of my faith. My experiences with Catholicism were so surreal that I never really got the faith thing.

Let me explain.

When I was a child, I'm talking four or five years old, the entire Sunday service was in Latin. Latin! To your average five-year-old, Latin is exactly the same as Martian. This church service was not designed to inspire faith in preschoolers. It was designed to give them nightmares.

The ceiling in Sacred Heart Church must be forty feet high. Every sound made at the altar reverberates from West Lynn to the shores of eternity.

My dad would dress us up like offerings and haul us into this strange world every Sunday. Soon some guy in a long robe and a giant hat would start to bellow and sing in the language of his native planet. We would all repeat these alien phrases in a group drone as we sat, knelt, or stood according to some incomprehensible agenda. No one ever said, "Now everyone sit; now everyone kneel." Somehow we just knew when to do these things. The big-hat guy would sing to us, "Domino skobisko etcum spirit tutu-o."

My brother and I were able to translate this phrase. It means, "The spaceship is coming."

Everything about the service was mysterious and indecipherable. Everything, that is, except God. He wasn't a complex mystical entity at all. He was an old guy with a big white beard. I know this because they had a huge painting of him on the ceiling above the altar.

When I wasn't standing on the kneeler, I couldn't see past the person seated in front of me, so I would look up at the Lord. He was sticking his head and torso out of some clouds, and he had the earth held tightly in his left arm.

God is a gigantic old man who lives in the clouds, speaks Martian, and holds the earth in a headlock.

Chapter Three
Confession

On Saturdays we would go to church and confess our sins. This activity took place in the smaller chapel downstairs. Normally you would find six or seven people sitting or kneeling in the pews adjacent to the confessionals awaiting their turn to unburden themselves of the week's accumulated crimes and misdemeanors.

It was a soul-cleansing assembly line of sorts.

If you, dear reader, are not Catholic and are struggling with the concept of confession, allow me to tell you the way it was explained to me when I was a child.

When you are born you may look like a sweet, innocent child of God, but the truth is that your soul is rotten and smelly from this thing called "original sin."

Because you are born a devil-child, your parents arrange to have your head dunked in some holy water to clean up your dirty little soul.

After your baptism, your soul is shiny, white, and neatly pressed like the shirt you wear to church on Sunday. Your parents love you and things are fabulous until you commit a sin.

Now, the word "commit" means to actually physically do something against the will of the big guy with the beard, but it is important to know that you also *commit* a sin at the exact moment that you *think* about committing one.

Sins stain your soul. They come in different shapes and sizes and some require more detergent (penance) to remove. For example, getting an erection when your teacher, Mrs. Hanlon, bends over to pick up an eraser from the floor would be like spilling a little grape soda on your shirt.

Showing it to her would be like spilling the entire bottle on your shirt.

And something on the order of being a pedophile priest would be like . . . well, just think of the most unpleasant thing you could do to soil a white shirt and that should give you an accurate visual image.

On Saturdays at Sacred Heart all these souls, in varying degrees of contamination, would line up for individual cleansing.

There were three lights above the confession booth. When a priest was in the booth a red light above the center would be lit. Red light on means "open for business."

There was a green light on each side of the red one that would turn on when you knelt down. Green light on means "sin cleaning in progress."

When it's your turn, you go in, kneel down, close the curtain behind you, and listen to the confession of the person on the other side. They're only three feet away. You can always hear them.

When the priest is done assigning an appropriate number of Hail Marys to the other sinner, he slides open a little speakeasy door and it's your turn.

You can't really see him, but you can make out his silhouette. It's like telling your sins to a shadow. You always start by saying, "Bless me father for I have sinned. It's been two weeks since my last confession."

It's very important to tell him how long it's been since you last confessed. Because he has to use an ancient sin-times-weeks-between-confessions sacred mathematical formula to ascertain what combination of prayers is required to wash away your current assemblage of crimes against God.

A soul that hasn't been through the wash for a month would naturally require a few more Acts of Contrition than one that comes back every week.

Then you tell him your sins. "Since then I lied, swore, and was disobedient to my parents and teachers. I also got a hard-on in school. For these and all my sins I am heartily sorry."

He gives you three Hail Marys, two Our Fathers and one Act of Contrition. You kneel at the altar, recite them quietly and presto! you walk out the door with a freshly cleaned, pressed, and neatly folded soul.

One of the arguments against confession is that it implies that the individual cannot speak directly to God.

This argument must have originated with a Unitarian.

Listen. If the God on the ceiling of your church is a hippie chick in a summer dress, you can ask her anything you want any time you feel like it because she's easygoing and not particularly vengeful.

We Catholics do not have a girly God. Our guy carries the whole earth around with him in a World Wrestling Federation headlock. If anyone ever had the audacity to ignore protocol and go over the priest's head to speak directly to the Almighty, God would reach over, give the earth a big noogie, and five thousand people would die in an earthquake in China.

I did not have any desire to talk to God. In fact, I liked the shadowy booth. It was like confessing over the phone.

A few times a year we would have these things called holy days of obligation. They would fall on weekdays and screw up the whole system.

For months you would be cruising along dirtying up your

soul from Monday to Friday and then running it through the Catholic car wash on Saturday so it would be clean enough for you to receive the body of Christ on Sunday.

Then along comes Ash Wednesday. You go to mass on Wednesday night and the priest dabs a glob of ashes on your forehead.

Maybe it's like getting your hand stamped at a nightclub. You know, a way for the guy at the door of the spaceship to know it's OK for you to come aboard.

There's this other holy day where you kneel at the altar and the priest blesses your throat by making a V shape with two candles and touching it to your neck. My best guess is that this is the Catholic version of a flu shot.

Anyway, there is a big problem with these holy days. You can't go to mass and receive communion on Wednesday night while your soul is carrying four days' worth of contamination from hopping freight trains, stealing cigarettes from your mother's purse, and having impure thoughts about every female that you ever met.

If they tried to put the body of Christ into the mouth of a soul this soiled, it would run away screaming.

So the Catholic authorities in their wisdom devised a solution.

I went to public school. After school on Tuesdays and Thursdays I would walk to the Catholic elementary school for an hour of religious instruction. On the Tuesday before a holy day of obligation they would line us all up in the hallway and one by one we would enter the principal's office, which had become a makeshift confessional.

I don't know what I expected when they told us that a priest was coming to the school to hear confession. I guess I hoped he would build a nice confessional in a dark corner of the basement so that I could enjoy the relative anonymity to which I had grown accustomed.

That was not the case.

I walked in and closed the door behind me. There, in the center of a very bright office, sat a priest. He was leaning back in a chair with his eyes closed. He was smoking a cigarette. The smoke rose up in a thin line from his hand and gathered in a large cloud above him.

This can't be right. I'm supposed to tell my sins to a whispering shadow, not some guy who's puffing on a weed with his eyes closed.

Oh how I longed for the darkness of the booth, the familiar silhouette behind the speakeasy door, the whispered penance.

This was icky.

What am I supposed to do here? Do I kneel down? I'm supposed to kneel, aren't I? No, just stand here and tell my sins?

Icky, icky, icky!

Less than a year after this experience, the smudge that adorned my forehead on Ash Wednesday was acquired from the cigarettes I had stolen from my mother's purse.

Chapter Four
Post 6

I never saw my Dad go to confession, but I always had the sense that he left mass on Sunday with a freshly cleaned soul. I think it had something to do with the fact that he was very generous with the weekly financial contribution he made to the church.

At a predetermined time toward the end of the service, a well-dressed man would walk down the aisle carrying what looked like a broom handle with a wicker basket attached to one end. He would stand at each pew and push it in front of everyone.

My siblings and I would each drop in the dollar that our father had given us. Dad, however, did not donate visible cash. When the basket paused before him, he would reach into the inside pocket of his suit coat and pull out a small pink envelope. It had a picture of Sacred Heart Church on it. Inside was an amount of money that would presumably embarrass the rest of the congregation were it not concealed.

The same soul purification acquired through confession by those of us who were less financially able seemed to me to be afforded in an expeditious manner to those members of the congregation (like my Dad) who possessed the monetary wherewithal.

Yes, boys and girls, you really can pay for your sins.

If God really loves a Catholic, he will have a truck run him over or a lightning bolt strike him in the short window of opportunity that exists between the time he confesses or pays for his sins and the time he starts dirtying up his soul again.

For my Dad this window of opportunity exists for approximately twelve minutes every Sunday. That is roughly how long it takes to drive from Sacred Heart Church to the bar in the basement of the American Legion Hall.

The life of my father is defined by a few key relationships. It is arguable that none is more significant than the one he has with the William P. Connery American Legion Post 6 on North Common Street in Lynn, Massachusetts.

Larry White is a veteran of World War Two and a full-blooded legionnaire. Post 6 is his place. Through the years his car has learned to drive there automatically. My dad would just get in, turn the key, shift into drive, and be transported there every day after work, every Wednesday night for Bingo, every Friday night to tend bar, every Saturday night for whatever, and *every single Sunday* after mass.

When we were young, the Post was still in the old wooden building. There was a new Legion Hall under construction next door, but the bar was still open in the basement of the old one.

Bars like Kenny's merely gave patrons the illusion of a subterranean world. Post 6 was the real thing. It was (and still is) actually underground.

The bar was small, one room. There was a faded mural of Iwo Jima on the wall. When you opened the door, you were then and are still to this day greeted by a smell that is unique to Post 6. It can't possibly be described. The best I can do is to say that it smells like the carpet had been soaked for years in beer, whiskey, cheap cigars, and the body odors of intoxicated old men.

My dad would give each of his children a dollar's worth of quarters. He would take a seat at the bar and we would run wild through the building.

In the summer months we would go outside and climb on the World War One cannon that sits in front of the building. We would use our quarters to play Beatles songs on the jukebox and to buy stale pistachios out of those dispensers that you crank your quarter into in return for three cents worth of the peanuts that turned your fingers and lips red.

Everyone, and I do mean everyone, smoked. If you

pressed the tip of your finger against a ceiling tile at Post 6 and then put it into your mouth, you would instantly overdose on nicotine.

Everyone, and I do mean everyone, drank alcohol. I'm talking about real-man World War Two alcohol—whiskey straight up. Beer only seemed to be on hand as a chaser.

This feels like a good time to document for posterity two quotes from Larry White on the subject of beer.

Quote number one:

"Beer? I wash my feet in it."

Quote number two:

"Beer? I drink that when I'm on the wagon."

In addition to smoking and drinking, the ancient, sacred art of gambling also found sanctuary in the bunker/bar beneath North Common Street.

And finally, Post 6 is a place where drunken sailors have always been able to feel at ease speaking like—well, drunken sailors.

Every Sunday of my childhood, within twelve magical minutes, my brother, sister, and I were transported from a building where sinful behavior (as in drinking, smoking, gambling, and cursing) was loathed and repented for, to the actual fountainhead of these activities.

It was awesome.

Chapter Five
Acting like an Asshole

The American legion is a club that requires membership. Technically, you have to be a war veteran to drink there. Members can bring in a guest. So over the years the unspoken rule for non-members has been: "You can drink here as long as you don't act like an asshole. If you don't know how to act, we will invoke the membership rule and your drinking privileges will be swiftly and unceremoniously terminated."

Now, "acting like an asshole" is a very elusive term. Not only does each bar have its own interpretation of what behavior will get you shut off or barred, but there are also different levels of what is considered sufferable behavior among the individual patrons.

If a regular patron who spends thirty dollars a day at Kenny's bar decides to hurl a barstool into the middle of Western Avenue, it's no big deal. He might even get a free drink out of it. But that same bartender would likely have a much lower tolerance for similar behavior from an occasional patron.

The same double standard exists between members and non-members of Post 6. As a non-member, if you spend money and keep quiet, they will tolerate your presence. But don't kid yourself. If there were enough members to keep the place jumping every night, you'd be drinking someplace else.

On the other hand, if you are a war veteran *and* a member, the threshold for what's considered acting like an asshole is a lot more loosely defined. In fact, if there actually was a level of obnoxious behavior that would get a Past Commander expelled from Post 6, I think Larry would agree that he would have discovered it many years ago.

So the rules on what it means to be acting like an asshole differ from bar to bar and are likely to have an equal degree of disparity among each bar's particular clientele, depending upon that patron's current position in the social hierarchy.

To further complicate the process, the social status of each patron in each bar is constantly in a state of flux, and each bartender brings to the job a different idea of what will be considered acceptable behavior during his or her shift.

The same behavior that will get you a pat on the back and a free beer at any given time in one venue, will get you barred for life in another.

The only thing that was certain in the West Lynn bar scene when I was a young man was that the establishment with the highest level of tolerance for uncivilized behavior was, without a doubt, Frank's.

Chapter Six
Frank's

There were three masses on Sunday morning at our church. The first was at 9:00 in the morning.

To my family, this mass was just a rumor. We saw it on the schedule but no one in our bloodline could verify that it ever really took place.

The third and last mass was at 12:00 noon.

Post 6 stopped serving alcohol at 2 AM on Sunday morning. The "High Noon Mass" seemed to me to have been created specifically for the families of the congregation for whom last call was the crowning achievement of Saturday night.

The parishioners who did not go out on Saturday night presumably went to the early morning Mass.

The teenage children of both groups told their parents that they were going to the 10:30 mass.

We were lying.

I did not enter gradually into the secret society of Irish Catholic teenage church skippers. I skipped church for the first time at the precise moment that I realized it was possible. I was barely thirteen.

By the time I was fourteen, I was something of a savvy veteran. At sixteen I would get up on Sunday morning and pretend to go to church just to avoid confrontation.

It was easier to walk the streets for an hour than to sleep in and incite a war at home. There was already plenty of verbal artillery being fired off in the Whites' house in those years. I was just doing my part to take the subject of church out of the equation.

Besides that, it was fun. A shadowy clan of Catholic teenagers killed the same hour in the doorways, in the playgrounds, and on the railroad tracks around the neighborhood every Sunday morning. It was a very exclusive social club.

Now that I think of it, it was like the bad kids' version of the CYO.

One Sunday morning in the summer of my sixteenth year, I met my new girlfriend down Barry Park. I was skipping church. She was not. She was too cool for that.

Just before one o'clock we walked out of the park and leaned against the wall of Frank's Bar. From there we had an excellent view of the front of the church so that I could see the people coming out and know when it was time to go home.

At the time, even though I had never set foot inside of Frank's, I knew that it was one the most dangerous bars in West Lynn. Everyone knew that it was a Wild West show in there because that was where all the craziest people in the city chose to imbibe.

In order to give you an example of the typical behavior that one might encounter in the company of the patrons of this legendary tavern, allow me to tell you about a ride home that my girlfriend once got from a couple of them.

She was eighteen and had just returned from seeing Howlin' Wolf at Sandy's Jazz Revival in Beverly. (Cool, huh? No giddy girls at that show.) It was one in the morning. She was walking home when a car pulled up beside her. Inside were two older guys that she knew from the neighborhood, Stevie Stone and Alan Sims. They offered her a ride home and she accepted.

As soon as she got in the car, she realized that these guys had been partying for days and were at the apex of the type of weekend adventure that was common among the people who frequented Frank's Corner Bar.

Let's take a moment here to discuss the word "partying." I may have been the oldest person in history to realize that this word does not mean the same thing to all people.

In 1988, after I had been dabbling in the Boston music scene for a while, I was invited to a party in Cambridge, Massachusetts, at the home of a folksinger.

I was thirty-one years old. I had been married for ten years and I had two children.

I swear to God that at that time in my life I had absolutely no idea that you could "party" in a way that did not include massive overconsumption of drugs and alcohol.

I went to this "party" and all the guests were sitting around sipping glasses of wine and engaging in conversation.

I thought I was in the wrong building.

I kept looking for a keg or a bathtub full of beer.

A typical weekend of partying, as I grew up understanding

it, would go something like this.

Phase One: On Friday afternoon you begin a massive intake of all available consciousness-altering substances. You continue this consumption through Phase Two, which consists of several hours of reckless abandon, until you arrive at Phase Three which occurs some time on Sunday and consists of any one or combination of the following:

Puking.

Fighting.

Passing out.

Crashing your automobile.

Having an exciting but potentially parole-violating interaction with local law enforcement.

So when I tell you that my future bride was in a car with two guys who had been partying for days, I do not mean that they had spent the first half of their weekend sipping wine and engaging in thought-provoking conversation.

They were, in the vernacular of the community, shitfaced.

She had unwittingly entered into the fully developed Phase Two section of a weekend party episode with two of the wildest people in the city.

They were going to give her a ride home, but first they were going to set a new world record in the speed and distance categories of the International Driving Backwards Competition in the Shit-Faced Olympics.

They took the small back road behind the America Park housing project toward a neighborhood near Saugus called Lynnhurst, driving backwards all the way. Then they pulled onto Walnut Street, which is one of the three main roads into the city.

Stevie drove at 40 MPH in reverse for three-quarters

of a mile laughing maniacally while she screamed at him to let her out. He drove backwards all the way to her house in Curwin Circle, let her out, and sped away.

*****

As we leaned against the side of Frank's Bar we began to see people coming out of church. The traffic soon came to a standstill and backed up for several blocks as streams of parishioners crossed Boston Street.

A city bus was caught in the line of traffic and was idling in front of Frank's.

As my girlfriend and I were standing there we saw Stevie and Alan emerge from a parked car across the street.

I think it's important to mention here that these were two very large men. They were, as was to be expected, at the tail end of what was undoubtedly another legendary weekend adventure. They began walking toward the bar, but could not resist the temptation to attack the bus first.

Now, you may ask, what exactly do you mean, Don White, when you say that they attacked the bus?

That is a fair question because, of all the many things I have seen in my life, this is the one and only time I have witnessed human beings attack a vehicle of public transportation.

They jumped up on the front bumper so their faces were against the windshield. They scowled and growled at the people inside. They pounded on the windows and the sides of the vehicle with their fists. Alan picked up a trashcan and threw it under the bus. Then he tore the cardboard advertising off the side and threw it into the street.

After several minutes, the horrified passengers watched

as Stevie and Alan waved and smiled at my girlfriend and then walked casually into the bar for a few drinks.

Chapter Seven
My Friend's Wedding

It was a beautiful Sunday in June back in the mid-1980s. My wife and I were getting ready to attend the wedding of the daughter of some close friends of my family.

I had an attitude problem.

I had built it on three inescapable facts:

1) I didn't have any clothes that were suitable to wear to a wedding, and I was doing the po' boy telephone scramble to try to borrow some. I knew from previous experience that no matter who loaned me their clothes I was still going to wind up looking like the bride's hillbilly cousin.

2) Even if I had a custom tailored suit to wear, there were fifty other things that I would rather do on a nice day in June.

3) I am a big fat whiney baby who hates weddings.

The ceremony was in the old chapel at Sacred Heart Church. My wife and I walked together up the steps, through the big wooden doors and into the church of our youth, she in a nice blue dress and I in my brother's pants.

We sat in a familiar wooden pew and looked around as people filtered in.

"What a great old building," I thought to myself. I looked up at the ceiling and there was the big guy. He didn't seem nearly as intimidating as I remembered him. He just looked kind of concerned and weary. It occurred to me that the grip he had on the earth might be less of an angry headlock and more of a protective embrace.

The parents of the bride had grown up with my mother and father. When we were young, we would see them at church on Sunday and later, after mass, we would run wild with their children at Post 6. Jimmy was the oldest. Dawn was next. It was her wedding that we were attending. Debra was the third child. She was born with multiple sclerosis and was wheelchair-bound. We only saw her when we visited them at their home. The youngest daughter was Diane.

The Church gradually filled up with my parents' friends and their extended families. It was a rare opportunity for me to see them all in one place. Soon, under the watchful eye of the big guy with the beard, I began to think about this tribe of mine.

All the elders were born just before or during the great depression. The elder men all had the experience of World War Two and the Korean conflict in common.

They were all Caucasian, mostly Irish with the occasional Italian or Polish family sprinkled in. And, of course, they were all Catholic.

Most of these people grew up dirt poor. I mean pre-food stamps, great-depression, empty-belly-in-the-classroom poor.

It defined them as much as anything else.

As I was watching them gather in the church, I began to feel like time had placed a gray film over my eyes to ensure that the black-and-white truths of my youth remained back in 1975 where they belonged.

Still, the eyes I was viewing them with now were not oblivious to the things they saw when I was a teenager. This tribe was essentially, to be brutally honest, a collection of intolerant, hypocritical, white alcoholics and their offspring. But these annoying new eyes of mine would not let me see a single person in the room without acknowledging and appreciating at least one extraordinary character trait per person.

It was infuriating.

When I looked at the priest that I knew was having an affair with a married woman, I could also see all the self-less work that he did for the homeless.

When I looked at the drunk who beat his wife, I also saw the war hero who saved the lives of three men in Korea.

When I looked at the guy that I had heard make racist remarks all my life, I also saw the guy who gave ten percent of his income to Catholic Charities, some significant portion of which went to people of color.

None of these positive attributes were really redeeming. They didn't do anything to alter the other character traits. It just seemed as if these good qualities had all decided that they were tired of being overshadowed by the obvious negatives and they were demanding to be acknowledged individually.

The ceremony was long and boring with a lot of mandatory Catholic aerobics (kneel, stand, sit, stand, sit, kneel, stand).

The reception was in the function room at the Nahant Country Club. On the ride over there I asked my wife if she knew the groom. She said she knew *of* him. I ask her what *of* him she knew? And she said:

"I know he was barred for life from Frank's."

At the time I was a regular patron of that venerable establishment. In fact, going there and getting drunk was at the top of my short list of things I would rather have done than go to this wedding. I had seen things take place in that bar room that no one would believe, behavior so brutally violent that it would sometimes cause me to long nostalgically for the comparably civilized days of the occasional attack on a bus.

My wife and I didn't speak as we drove down the causeway to Nahant. I was busy running through a list in my mind of my top ten most unbelievable Frank's memories. I selected individual categories for viewing.

The most violent.

The most obscene.

The most insane.

The most intoxicated.

The most felonious.

These categories each had subsections that featured impressive cross-references which combined key ingredients of the most violent, most obscene, and most intoxicated files.

I called them up one after another and as the sober light of reflection shone upon the brutality and absolute insanity of each one, my astonishment continued to grow.

Finally, I threw my hands up and blurted out, "What in the name of God would a person have to do to get barred from Frank's?"

I entered the reception with a sense of awe. This was no ordinary groom.

Under normal circumstances I would have begun my whining big-fat-baby-who-hates-weddings routine into the ear of my wife right after dinner with the intention of wearing her down into an early departure.

But on this day I chose not to do that because I was preoccupied by my fascination with the groom. He seemed so normal.

I kept trying to picture this clean-shaven, tuxedoed young man participating in the unspeakable activities that I thought might possibly justify excommunication from Frank's Bar.

Chapter Eight
Disco Illumination

After dinner people began to filter onto the dance floor. I watched silently. With all the thoughts of the day regarding the complexities of my tribe still fresh and swirling in my mind, I was half expecting to be the recipient of some sort of significant illumination. An hour later a truth, of which I had been entirely oblivious, was, in fact, revealed to me. The interesting thing about this revelation was that it was completely unrelated to anything that I had thought about all day. It was a revelation about disco music.

I love music. I especially love lyrics. My musical hero is Frank Zappa. I count among my influences in the field of lyric writing Bob Dylan, Paul Simon, Tom Waits, and John Prine.

Up until the time of my disco illumination I stood resolutely on the "disco sucks" side of the opinion field. In addition to my disdain for what I felt were feloniously termed "lyrics" in this "music" I feel I should also mention that I don't dance.

Don't.

Can't.

Won't.

Whatever.

Just not comfortable doing it.

I am however, quite comfortable watching other people doing it. (Dancing, that is.) I especially enjoy watching bad dancing.

I recall a poorly attended folk concert that took place on a gazebo on Boston Common. There may have been thirty people there—half of whom were performers. I was standing beside Mr. Walt Thompson who is an extraordinary musician, singer, and writer of songs. For the purpose of this vignette it is also important to note that he is an African American and the possessor of a notorious barbed wit.

A mediocre banjo and guitar instrumental from a duo on the gazebo had instigated a dance frenzy among the folk fans in attendance—a frenzy that was . . . epileptic in nature. As I stood beside Mr. Thompson thinking of ways by which, if need be, I might be able to keep these dancers from swallowing their tongues, he leaned over and whispered this question into my ear:

"How on earth do you people reproduce?"

Watching bad dancing is like watching slapstick.

Watching good dancing is something altogether different.

As much as I hate weddings I must admit that I am always fascinated with what takes place on the dance floor at the receptions.

A half dozen teenage girls were the first to lay claim to the hardwood real estate at the center of the banquet hall. Under the banner of safety in numbers they all danced together. A bit gangly, they each seemed to overcompensate for the lack of sureness in their steps with just a little too much laughter.

The dance floor was their exclusive domain for the

next twenty minutes. Meanwhile the people with whom they would soon share this space were consuming alcohol and talking louder with each intervening minute.

Single women in their twenties were the next demographic to set their sights on the dance floor. They seemed to me to be of an entirely different species than the current occupants. Where the teenage girls had bounced arm in arm onto the floor, this group approached slowly, steadily.

I watched and thought that if allowed to take its natural course, the ten years between age fifteen and age twenty-five will sculpt the adolescent raw material of a young woman into something elegant and completely unrecognizable to its predecessor. In each of their steps I see the experience of love, heartbreak, passion, and loss, and the passage of just enough time to process and incorporate each.

Simply put, grace has made its first appearance on the dance floor.

Later, when a torch song from the nineteen-forties is played, grace unveils her journeymen.

Four couples—all grandparents—take the floor and begin waltzing before me.

I suddenly long for eyes with less vision—eyes that see only what is plainly before them. Instead, my cursed portals, that only moments ago were showing me the passion and heartache in the steps of young women, are now completely overloading my sensory system with all that is spoken within the movements of a collective two hundred years of matrimony.

With each unified step in three-quarter time comes a tidal wave containing all the pain and joy that having built a life and raised a family with another person can bring. I lean back in my chair defenseless. I have no choice but to let it all wash over me. I am drowning in a flood of images. As I am about to go down for the third time, the song ends, grace re-veils her journeymen, and the DJ plays a Little Richard song. I then add my name to the long list of persons whose lives have been saved by those sacred words:

Wop bop a lu bop a wop bam boom!

The young men are drunk now. They attack the dance floor and instantly defoliate grace's garden. What had only seconds before been a waltzing testimonial to elegance now resembles a boxing ring.

The girlfriends of these intoxicated stallions are swept up into their gravitational pull. The sure-footed magnificence with which these young women once ruled the dance floor seems a distant memory. Their participation in the pugilist dance has reduced them in my eye to little more than sparring partners.

I am resentful and begin to plot my escape.

It is then that the first notes of the disco song begin to blare from the speakers. All conversations with women of child-bearing age are abruptly halted as if a hypnotist had spoken the trigger word and these women had all snapped back under his spell. From every corner of the hall there is a mad dash to the dance floor.

I watch in astonishment as the center of the room becomes a sea of writhing, grinding, pulsating, extremely creative, simulated fornication. It is a giant fertility dance and the participants are helpless. They must do what the disco gods command. Do a little dance. Make a little love. Get down tonight.

What a fool I have been. I thought Bob Dylan was a genius. What planet had I been living on for all those years?

At best, a song of his might induce a driblet of erogenous moisture in the small percentage of women in the world for whom a clever turn of phrase unleashes sexual desire. With a little luck a carefully selected Bob Dylan song might get your art student girlfriend to light a couple of candles and permit you to gently make love to her—provided that you recite an appropriately romantic poem first. This is genius? I think not.

The person who can write a song that commands every woman at a wedding reception between eighteen and forty to present a real-time simulation of the exact methods by which she could fuck you sideways, upside down, and into a coma, if she so desired, is, without a doubt, the greatest songwriting genius in the history of the world and my personal hero.

It is a significant revelation in the mind of a serious writer that causes Bob Dylan to be dethroned by KC and the Sunshine Band.

Chapter Nine
The Five Minutes

At the time of her sister's wedding, Debra was twenty-one. Two decades of multiple sclerosis had twisted her into this tiny, contorted young woman. She sat in her wheelchair at a table with her family near the dance floor.

The muscles in her neck had long ago surrendered the fight to keep her head held up. Her head rested upon her shoulder giving her, I thought, a skewed view of the proceedings.

As the party was winding down the DJ played a slow song—another waltz. I watched the groom walk over to Debra. He bent down, tucked his two hands under her arms and lifted her out of the wheelchair. Her legs stayed curled up beneath her as he carried her onto the dance floor. Her chin rested upon his shoulder.

The floor cleared. Everyone stopped and watched. When the groom's back was to our table, we could see Debra's face, set upright atop his shoulder, and looking wide-eyed around the room. Her body was hidden from our view.

It would have been easy to picture her face attached to a young healthy girl moving perfectly in step with him except that her face could not conceal her lifetime in a wheelchair.

Both of Debra's sisters are absolutely gorgeous. They are petite, fair-skinned, and stunning. It seems reasonable to assume that they each have had more than their fair share of attention from young men.

I pictured the perfectly coherent and articulate girl behind Debra's eyes peering out at a world that routinely bestowed upon her sisters all the experiences that mark the stages of a girl's journey to adulthood.

She was sitting in her wheelchair when her sisters went out on their first dates, when they went to and returned from the prom. And here she was again today at Dawn's wedding.

This face that looked at us from the shoulder of her dance partner was that of a young woman who had spent her life silently watching as the dreams of other people came true.

This was a face that never expected to be beautiful.

Now, through the spontaneous action of her newly anointed brother-in-law, for five minutes at her sister's wedding, and for the only time in her life, she was the belle of the ball.

She ruled the dance floor with the handsomest man in the building.

She was, in the eyes of everyone in attendance, and presumably in her own mind, quite simply the most beautiful woman in the world.

She looked to me as if she would burst.

When the music stopped, the man who was barred for life from Frank's Corner Bar placed her gently back into her wheelchair, kissed her on the forehead, and disappeared into the crowd.

Moments

"Do you want to get up and say goodbye?"

I said, "I'll see him next weekend." But the part of my head that understands the value of moments slapped the part of my head that would choose an extra hour of sleep over an extra year of life and then insisted that I put on a pair of pants and go downstairs.

The longer you live the more of these moments you have. You know, the ones that seem to contain within them every emotion that you have ever felt. And after their whirlwind has subsided, the way that you have been living is permanently altered, relegated to the memory department, and thereafter described in sentences that begin with phrases like: "When I was still in high school . . . Before I started working nights . . . When the kids were small . . . Prior to that episode with Monica . . ."

So I got out of bed and set into motion the process that would close the era of what will henceforth be referred to as "Before Lawren went to college."

He was born in the second-floor bedroom of a house in Maine that featured such amenities as cold running water (summertime only) and a two-seat outhouse (a big hit among my visiting relatives). At birth he wore the face of an ancient. He looked to me like an old sage who was arriving to take care of some special business that couldn't be trusted to underlings.

I am sitting in the chair in the living room. I am surveying. Lawren and his mother are taking care of last-minute packing. The scene is identical to several I have seen in the past in which he was preparing to go away for the weekend—identical except for the stress on the faces of the players in today's performance. His sister is waking up slowly. The big goodbye is imminent. When I was younger, and these moments came and went, I assembled their significance and magnitude in retrospect—often years later. But I'm all here for this one. In my mind I am running my fingertips over the faces of a hundred snapshots of my eighteen-year relationship with this young man—each one significant because it represents a key instance of growth for one or both of us. These are the moments that have collectively conspired to bring us, whether I am emotionally prepared or not, to this one.

I ask him to play the Beethoven piece on the piano that he has filled our home with daily for the past year. He is nervous. This is making it too real. He mutilates the piece. It is the most beautiful thing I have ever heard. I am crying. He hugs his sister. She is crying and goes upstairs. His mother waits till he is in the car, then looks at me as if to say that my lack of composure is a direct threat to her role as emotional empress of the family. She wells up, reclaiming her title, and we laugh/cry. She plucks a bottle of Motrin off the counter saying that the entire contents might be enough to get her through the day. We laugh/cry again and they are gone.

I sit in the chair and marvel at how alive I am. I am the alivest person on earth. There is so much emotional electricity running through me that I could probably start my car by sticking my finger in the ignition. I am squeezing the final seconds out of one of those moments that defies you to question the meaning of life. I can hear it saying, " If you can actually muster up the massive amount of ignorance necessary to raise the question of life's meaning during a moment that has placed you among the most alive people on earth, I'm afraid there's not much I can do for you."

I am living a very full life. I have had the privilege of countless exhilarating moments on stage. Moments so powerful that during them I have actually felt removed from the constraints of time. I have had moments of such dreamy euphoria during the composing of certain pieces that it has occurred to me at these times that I might possibly be reversing the aging process. (This seems to be balanced nicely by the acceleration of the process that takes place during the composing of the crappy songs.) In any case, I know how lucky I am. What I am realizing (and some part of me has known this all along) is that these highs that have to do with music are great, but all of them combined are not qualified to sit at the same table with the experience that I am sharing with you here today.

I am going to stop short of actually thanking the people in the music business who have overlooked me with impressive consistency through the years. (Sarcasm: one of my most enjoyable but less enviable gifts.) But if I had had early success in the business and spent the bulk of the past ten years on the road, the depth of my experience today would have been profoundly diminished. And any behavior on the part of any person that, directly or indirectly, contributed to my being able to drink so deeply of life is, I suppose, worthy of some thanks.

Take care of your special business old sage. It has been a privilege to help raise you. You are one of the most remarkable human beings I have ever known.

There will be other moments for us.

Thank you for this one.

Father's Day

When my children were small, we lived on the ground floor of what is locally called a three-decker—a wooden three-story house with a rental apartment on each floor. The building had a garage behind it that belonged to the landlord.

I came home from work one afternoon very tired. My wife met me in the driveway and told me that my five-year-old son had broken the window in the garage. He hadn't broken it by accident. He just threw rocks at it until it broke.

At the time I was working for a security company as a residential alarm system installer. It was midsummer and I had spent the entire day running wires in the attic of an old home. It must have been 120 degrees up there. There was no floor and the space between the floor joists was filled with that old lambs-wool type of insulation. All day long every step I took and everything I touched released great toxic plumes of dust and insulation. It was the kind of day that makes a man think that he probably should have studied harder in school. I was hot, sweaty, itchy, hungry, and a few steps beyond borderline homicidal.

I stood with my shoulders slumped and my head hung down as my wife filled me in on the details of my son's heinous crime. I felt like a man who has been tortured for so long that he is willing to give up all his nation's secrets provided that his reward for doing so is a quick death. My wife's words were being processed and analyzed by a brain that had begun this day as a fine-tuned V8 engine, but was now limping forward on two cylinders. One cylinder was processing information and the other was imagining my wife and I sipping margaritas on a tropical beach.

This was the first time I ever recall being on the adult side of the "wait till your father gets home" thing.

I reached down into my energy reservoir, felt my knuckles scrape the bottom of the tank, and managed to pull up the last usable handful. I straightened my back, lifted my head, and approached the scene of the crime. All the while dreaming of the hot water bathtub submersion that awaited the resolution of this day's last job.

I was standing before the broken window and calculating the cost of repairing it when I felt my son's presence behind me. I turned my head and saw him standing near the back porch. He was wearing a face that triggered an avalanche of undefined emotions in me, emotions unleashed so fast and furiously into my diminished brain that I simply could not process them.

When I saw this look on my son's face I decided to take some time to think the situation through before acting. Without speaking to him I went into the apartment and filled the bathtub. With the temperature of the water in the vicinity of boiling I climbed in and slowly submerged. As the hot water drew from my body the day's sweat, dirt, and insulation fibers, a few old memories were drawn out as well.

1967:

I was ten years old. A little leaguer. The Boston Red Sox were on their way to their first trip to the World Series since the Ted Williams era. I was obsessed with baseball. Earlier that summer I had pitched the final three innings of the championship game for my little league team. I struck out Jimmy Jacobs with the bases loaded to give us a thirteen to twelve victory and the pennant. I was carried off the field by my teammates as all my friends and family looked on.

I had every baseball card of every team in the American League. I would turn my living room into Fenway Park and play nine-inning games with them. Home plate was in front of the chair near the window. The couch was the green monster. I would spread my cards on the floor in the shape of a baseball diamond. I had a shoe box full of little scraps of paper. Each piece of paper had something written on it: single, double, triple, home run, ground out, fly out, pop up, strike out. I even had a bunt and a balk in there. I would shake up the box and play nine innings by moving baseball cards around the floor of my living room field according to what was written on the scraps of paper that I pulled out. I was the baseballingest ten-year-old in America.

On Summer afternoons my baseball addiction would take me to the back yard. There was a patch of dirt and gravel near our back steps where no grass ever grew. I would stand there facing the lawn and with my old Al Kaline bat in hand I would hit rocks out toward the street. If the rock stayed in the yard it was an out. If it went over the hedges and the white picket fence onto Fuller Street it was a single. Across the street to the opposite sidewalk meant extra bases and anything into the Ceceres' yard or off their house was, obviously, a home run. Any rock that landed behind the tree in right field or hit the Nicholsons' house in left was foul. I played this game all summer. I was always true to the current Red Sox line up. I even hit my rocks from the left side of the plate for Carl Yastremski.

At the beginning of the season there was a seemingly unlimited supply of pebbles at home plate. Pebbles were perfect for this game, because even back-to-back home runs off the Ceceres' house from the heart of the Red Sox batting order could barely be heard inside above the sound of the radio the Cecere kids were always playing.

The baseball season is long. Every team has to overcome several challenges during the course of 162 games: injuries, fatigue, slumps, and, of course, a dramatic reduction in the availability of quality pebbles.

In May and June I was standing on pebbles. I would just reach down and grab a perfect almond-sized one to toss up in the air and swat toward the street. Come August I was scratching around in the dirt with my bat between every pitch and unearthing something more crabapple-size.

Man on first one out—Rico Petrocelli up. Here's the pitch. It looks like a miniature asteroid. It's about five inches long and two inches wide with a thirty degree bend in the middle. Rico is expecting a fast ball and is way out in front of the curve. He hooks it to left—a bullet over the Yankees' dugout and into the stands.

Crash!

Yes little Donnie White, everything *is* peaceful in your pastoral baseball fantasyland but back here in reality you just broke the Nicholsons' bathroom window.

Shit!

"Hit the showers kid, your season just ended."

There were six windows on the side of the Nicholsons' house that faced Don White Field. If Rico Petrocelli was so determined to drive a miniature asteroid through one of them, you'd think he could have at least picked one of the five standard ones. No. He had to smash the irreplaceable stained glass one.

"Wait till your father gets home."

My old man worked as a rigger at the General Electric plant. In 1967 he was forty years old.

Now, as I lay there simmering in my bathtub, beneath a steam cloud of sweat, insulation, and memories, I recalled him coming home from work that day and being accosted in the driveway by my mother with the lurid details of the baseball asteroid incident. I then added to my collection of identifiable facial expressions that of a man coming to grips with the fact that the closing of the gate behind him in his driveway does not necessarily guarantee the end of his work day.

My parents grew up in a time when people hit their kids. It is comforting for me to know that, without any help or guidance, they had decided not to discipline their children in that manner. This has always seemed to me like a major move forward in the evolution of the bloodline.

They didn't hit me. They yelled at me. They told me how stupid it was to hit rocks with a baseball bat. My dad paid for a new window and they both stayed angry with me for about a week. During that week they gave me the cold shoulder. It was as if they had made a list of things that they were obligated to do for me. "Feed him." "Wash his clothes." "Bring him to church." But make sure that this ten-year-old knows, at least for a while, his dad is not his pal.

"Dad, I cleaned up the cellar today. I put all your paint cans and brushes into this cabinet."

"Fine." He walks away. Message clear: not your pal.

I think I might have preferred to be hit.

After my bath I opened the door and emerged from the thoughtful steam. I was cleansed and reinvigorated. I was prepared to take up the reins and do my part to move my section of this ridiculous genealogy forward.

I measured the window. I called the McCarthy Glass Company. They told me that it would cost five dollars to cut a new pane of glass and a dollar fifty for a can of putty. They also told me that they would be open for two more hours.

My son was in his room. He was sitting on the bottom bunk staring at the wall. He was wearing the second identifiable facial expression that I would log into my collection that day—that of a person who messed up and was sure that there was nothing he could do to make it better.

I said, "Come on, let's go look at the window." It turned out to be a longer walk than I expected. My left ankle was chained to my points of reference. They were heavy. I dragged them along and used the time to ponder them.

When I had broken the Nicholsons' window my parents had chosen not to knock me upside the head. They were able to remember how that felt when they were kids and they made a conscious decision to discipline their children without physical violence.

When my son broke the landlord's window I recalled how awful it felt to be given the cold shoulder by my parents, so naturally I hauled off and punched him in the nose.

I'm kidding.

In my community, it is not uncommon for the meager evolutionary steps taken with enormous pains in one generation to be carelessly dismantled by the next. But I was determined to build upon the accomplishments of those who came before me.

Somewhere in my adult life, when facing a big decision, I had gotten into the habit of picturing my family history through the eyes of someone viewing it three hundred years in the future. That person would see me as a man who lived for a certain amount of time in the middle of the lineage. As I pondered my choices, I would try to imagine how these decisions would look in the context of my overall genealogy. Ideally, an objective genealogist would be able to point to my small time segment and say something like: "This is where the adult males in the family stopped handing down the gift of alcoholism to their offspring."

Unfortunately, this exercise has not always produced the most desirable long-term results. On the cusp of several important decisions over the years I have been known to say, "All genealogists from the year 2290 can go fuck themselves," and then proceed to march headlong into the decision that would bring me the greatest immediate pleasure.

However, as I walked toward the broken window with my points of reference in tow and this unhappy little boy beside me, I pictured a man in a suit, alone in a library, looking up from a book of my family history and saying, "The practice of empowering the children to take responsibility for the sincere and timely resolution of their mistakes was introduced into this bloodline by Don White in 1985. With a few noteworthy exceptions, this character trait can still be observed in his descendants today."

At the crime scene I said to my son, "You made a pretty big mistake today." His eyes welled up. It caught me by surprise. It made me realize how big the world looks from three feet off the ground. I pulled over a milk crate that was next to the garage and sat down so he wouldn't have to look up at me as if I was a giant. One essential tool for empowering little people is to demystify big people. The first phase of the demystification process is to un-giant yourself. The second is to tell the truth.

"I make mistakes," I told him. "I make them all the time. You know how I feel when I make a mistake? I feel like crap. I don't just feel like regular crap. I feel like great big piles of steamy dog crap." He can't help it—he laughs. Nothing eases the tension of a five-year-old who has the weight of the world on his back quite like a little poo-poo joke from his dad. "I hate how I feel after I make a mistake, don't you?" He nodded his head in agreement. "Do you want me to tell you what I do that makes me feel good again after I have made a big mistake?" He looked at me with big round blue eyes that said, "If you are telling me sir, that there is actually a way for me to be a happy child again, then yes indeed, I am very interested. Please, do go on."

I bit my tongue, and with all my limited intestinal fortitude, I resisted the temptation to say, "First you take the rent money, go to the corner bar and spend it on alcohol and cocaine. Nine hours later, after you have cheated on your wife with someone whose name you don't know, contracted a social disease, smashed up the family car and been arrested for driving under the influence, believe me little dude, this broken window won't mean shit."

Not unlike much of my humor, this would have been funny, but inappropriate and counterproductive.

Instead I said, "Your dad has two rules about mistakes. First, try not to make the same one over and over again (a rule, I must admit, with which I have had varying degrees of success), and second, whenever possible reach in your pocket and pay to fix the damage." I watched his face change from that of a kid who thought he was about to learn how to reclaim his happiness to one that said, "I'm five years old. How am I supposed to pay to fix this mistake? Thanks for nothing asshole." I said to him, "It will cost six dollars and fifty cents to buy the new glass and a can of putty to fix this window. I bet you have at least that much in your piggy bank. Your mother has some penny rolls in the top drawer in the pantry. If you roll up six-fifty worth of coins, I will take you to the glass place to buy a new pane of glass and I will help you fix the window."

Though I suspected that I might be doing something useful here for the little dude, it wasn't until I saw the look on his face and felt my ankle unleashed from my points of reference that I began to glimpse the potential of Daddy Don's Little Dude Empowerment Program. As my proposal began to sink in, I watched this simple idea transform him from helpless, hopeless, and miserable to a small man on a mission. He bolted into the house.

What I called his piggy bank was actually a Dukes of Hazzard car. There wasn't a lot of money in the White household in those days. Our children didn't have a lot of toys. In order to get at his money he had to destroy his car by cutting it open. He sat on the living room floor staring at the car and holding the big scissors that would be used to cut open the roof. His mother and I leaned against the wall and watched as he grappled with the decision at hand.

My son loved his Dukes of Hazzard car. It sat on his

bedroom bureau. It was the last thing he saw when he went to sleep and the first thing he saw in the morning. It was the envy of his friends. It made him feel special.

This was difficult for me to watch. I was close to saying, "You know, put the bank back on your bureau. I'll buy the new window," when he picked the scissors up off the floor, handed them to me and said, "Break it open Dad. I want to fix my own mistake."

I cut the roof off the car. He spilled the contents out onto the living room floor. We rolled up the bulk of his life savings and drove to the McCarthy Glass Company.

The woman who worked there was a classic grandmother type in her early sixties. The counter she stood behind was twelve inches taller than my son. She watched with amused curiosity as a small hand appeared above the front of the counter and dropped a roll of pennies on top of it. After the tiny hand had disappeared and returned to deposit more penny rolls, a nickel roll, and a small handful of dimes and quarters, she leaned forward to view the boy who was attached to this mysterious appendage and said, "Well now, what do we have here?"

My son said nothing so I said, "He made a mistake today and broke the garage window. He felt really bad and decided that he would take responsibility for it and fix it himself with his own money."

Her eyes met mine and in that split second she communicated a complete understanding of the scene. She was prepared to deliver her part in this play flawlessly. She brought her face down close to his and said, "Well, aren't you just the most wonderful young man? Not too many children your age would do what you're doing." She looked up at me and with a barely perceptible wink she said, "This is a very special child you have here. You must be very proud of him. I think he deserves a reward."

And like a magic trick, a purple lollipop appeared in her hand. She placed it in his shirt pocket and in a warm grandmotherly voice, almost a whisper, she said, "You should feel really good about yourself."

Bravo! She nailed it.

In my mind, the curtain came down and then opened again to reveal my son, the grandmother character and I holding hands in front of the glass company stage scenery and bowing in unison to thunderous applause.

It probably doesn't really take a whole village to raise a child, but an occasional serendipitous command performance from a stranger behind a counter can be very helpful.

On the ride back to the apartment, my son sat on the front seat beside me. The new pane of glass he had purchased was wrapped neatly in brown paper between us. The can of putty was in a small paper bag on his lap. On the ride to McCarthy Glass his shoulders had been slumped and he looked old and world-weary. Now he was taller. He looked good—like a kid again. It made me happy.

*****

On Father's Day I called my dad and told him that I'd like to take him out for lunch. He didn't want to do it. A month before, I had stormed into his kitchen while he was having breakfast. I then spent ten minutes screaming at him. I had condensed thirty-five years of unspoken feelings on the subject of everything that sucked about having him as a father into those tumultuous minutes. My verbal volcanic eruption froze him at the table. He sat there holding a fork with a piece of egg on it and stared at me. It was not an experience he was anxious to repeat again any time soon.

I sensed his understandable lack of enthusiasm and assured him that I was quite satisfied with the emotional cleansing I had induced for myself during his breakfast. I therefore felt no need to subject him to any further litanies of his paternal shortcomings as I perceived them.

Reluctantly, he agreed to come.

I picked him up and brought him to a local restaurant/ bar called the Shawmut. As we were being seated I remembered a story that my mother had told me about my dad when he was a kid.

His father was the type of alcoholic that would get paid on Friday and spend his whole paycheck at the bar that night. When my dad was a young man he used to go to the bar and try to get his old man to go home before he spent all the money. I had often pictured him riding his bike home after having failed to instill, through his pleading, any consideration for the family into his father's consciousness. I could see him, pedaling hard on his bike and promising himself that he would not forget how he felt and that his kids would never have to feel this way.

The bar where my grandfather drank on Fridays after work was the Shawmut.

The place was full of ghosts from 1938. As we looked over the luncheon menu they hovered around us, curious to see what had become of the kid with the bicycle. I wanted them to know, so during our lunch I proceeded to tell my dad (loud enough for his hovering ghosts to hear) everything that I admired about the way he chose to live his life.

I said: "Your father drank all the money and left you guys with nothing, but you always made sure that we had plenty of food and a nice place to live. At thirteen years old you had to become the breadwinner in your family. Thanks for giving me the teenage years that you never had. Even though you had to assume the role of provider at the price of your own childhood, you never held it against your father. There is a deep sense of forgiveness at the core of you that is very impressive to me. Thanks for that, Dad. I'm sorry for saying all those things to you last month. That wasn't really about you. It was about me. I just needed to say them one time to make sure they didn't lie around and fester inside me. The truth is that you and Ma both handed me a life that was so much better than the lives you were handed. You're a great guy. I love you a lot and all the ghosts in this place can go to hell." He looked at me kind of confused and said, "What was that last thing you said?"

I said, "Oh . . . just forget that part.

"I love you.

"Happy Father's Day."

The Viking Ship

My stomach hurts.

This subject makes me ill. I would rather talk about anything —lawn care, the current infidelities of the characters on General Hospital, anything but this. On these rare occasions when I force myself to look back at my double-decade dance with drugs and alcohol, all I can think about is the magnitude of what I failed to accomplish during those years.

Oooh, I'll be back in a sec. I gotta go take some Mylanta.

*****

Man, that stuff is magic. OK, where were we? Right, the drug years. Well, they sucked.

The End.

*****

All right, all right, I'll do it. Not because I want to. Believe me, I don't.

(Triumphant, Hollywood-style, overcoming-tragedy musical soundtrack begins and Don speaks over the music.)

But maybe, just maybe, one of my little stories about what a complete asshole I have been in my life might, in some small way, help some other selfish and inconsiderate drug addict justify his past behavior by copping out and attributing it all to destiny . . .

(The triumphant music ends abruptly at this moment as if someone has unplugged the tape machine.)

What the hell am I talking about?

I'll tell you.

For some reason, I have become a homing beacon for people who have an incurable need to speak the following words.

"You know, Don, everything that we have done in our lives, every decision, good and bad, was exactly what was necessary to bring us to the place we are today."

These people need a beating. And if I understand their philosophy correctly, I could actually pummel them mercilessly today and reflect upon it later as something that was necessary to bring me to the wonderful place that I'd be reflecting from.

As far as I am concerned those words I quoted are just a way for people in recovery to make themselves feel better about all the unnecessary pain and suffering they caused while they were strung out.

Yes, I am at a fabulous place in my life. And yes, I actually did get to this fabulous place via the road I took to get here.

Duh.

Could I have taken a shorter road to my present life? Could I have made decisions along the way that might have shaved a few years off of my eighteen-year sabbatical from productivity? Could I have chosen to hurt a few less people along the way?

Yes, yes, and yes.

Did I?

Nope.

Why?

Addicts are assholes, that's why. It's really not any more complicated than that.

I have chosen to keep the memories from that time in my life alive and accurate because it helps me to remember why I prefer not to return there. I think that regrets are totally unappreciated in today's society. Stop demonizing your regrets. They are your friends, embrace them.

On the not-so-rare occasions when I find myself performing manual labor in a hot, toxic workspace, and my lungs are filling up with some unpronounceable poison that is gnawing an hour off the end of my life with each inhalation, I am often visited by one of my most persistent regrets. I call him Party Boy. He's sixteen years old. He bears a striking resemblance, both physically and in his view of the world, to myself at his age. He knows everything, and he's skipping school to go to a keg party.

He and I have this little game we like to play where he gets a lot of enjoyment out of taunting me and I get equal pleasure from threatening to kill him. It's great fun.

He will pop his head into my crawlspace and find me with my cranium stuffed into the fiberglass insulation at the side of the attic where the roof meets the open floor. My body is drenched in sweat. All the loose fibers that he has made airborne with the insertion of his perky face into my work area are slowly floating toward me and sticking to my soppy brow as if it were a freshly tilled garden for the planting of fiberglass seeds.

"Hey dude," he says, "there's a big keg party up the woods today. I know you've got two exams this afternoon, but fuck it, school is for losers. What does algebra have to do with the real world anyway? Besides, we're gonna be rock stars. The only math a rock star needs to know is how many grams are in an ounce of coke."

I will respond (cough, wheeze, hack, puke), "C'mere you fuckin' idiot. No, I'm not gonna hurt you, just climb up in here for a minute and tell me some more about this party. It sounds great." Then he'll say, "No way, dude. You just want to squeeze my throat until I can't breathe any more, as if that could turn back time." Then, after he has taken a long look at the impressive workspace that I have made manifest in order to earn a living, a mischievous, borderline diabolical grin will slide across his face and he will say, "You know something dude, everything that we have done in our lives, every decision, good and bad, was exactly what was necessary to bring us to this amazing place we are today."

I appreciate my wise-ass regrets and I prefer them in their natural state without the candy coating, because I want the occasional swallowing of these pills to remain as bitter as possible.

So, rather than trying to justify my past, I just keep it on file with all the horrendous missteps intact. And when in the course of my life it becomes necessary to go back and take a look at my past, my behavior does not seem like the only road that could lead me to the life I now have. It seems more like the reason it took so long to get here. This reflection sucks and it hurts my stomach, but it helps to ensure that my future decision making will be more likely to contain a healthy dose of circumspection . . . and, I suppose, an equally healthy dose of Mylanta.

*****

I am resisting the temptation here to describe a handful of truly unbelievable incidents from this period of my life. I'm sure that they would make for very engaging reading, but I hate them. I mean I *really* hate them. Don't get me wrong, they're among the best stories I have. They have every ingredient that is essential to hold the attention of even the most A.D.D. inflicted reader—out-of-control characters, abysmal decision making, mind-boggling overconsumption of exotic illicit substances, car chases, tension-building cat and mouse games with poorly-written, one-dimensional local police officers. These years of my life harbor story lines that are perfect for at least a half a dozen mediocre made-for-television movies. But I'm afraid you're going to have to wait until I am on the edge of starvation before I intention-ally glorify these memories in writing, because to me they are all just stories about getting away with it or not getting away with it. I do not find them interesting.

I am willing, however, to do two things here. I will describe in detail the end of one all-night cocaine and alcohol binge and I will also tell the story of how I finally quit for good. Then I will close the door on this subject and move on.

*****

Of all the stupid places in the world to be, inside the mind of an addict is by far the stupidest.

There is a sign on the road when you enter an addict's mind that says:

> ENTERING ALTERNATE UNIVERSE
> NRNA
> (NO REASON NEED APPLY)
> LEAVE YOUR GOOD JUDGMENT AND
> COMMON SENSE AT THE BORDER

Beneath these words is the letter L inside a circle with a line going through it, the universal sign for No Logic.

Under the rule of King Richard the Third (known to his many loyal subjects as Rick Diculous), this is the Land of Opposites. There is only one rule here: anything is justifiable as long as it serves to maintain the flow of whatever it is that you are addicted to.

Anything that persons outside the Land of Opposites would consider reason will, of course, be the first victim of this rule.

Here it is perfectly reasonable to spend your children's birthday money on drugs. When accused of being a selfish asshole, it is also reasonable (under the Rick Dick rules of engagement) to blame the person who points this out to you. Wait, it gets better. You are further justified—no, *obligated*—to raise your voice in convoluted righteous indignation and tell anyone who dares to confront you that the reason you drink and take drugs stems directly from the fact that they are always bitching at you. It doesn't matter that this is a lie.

It doesn't matter how ridiculous it sounds. It doesn't even matter that your response to their accusation actually proves that they are right. Because right or not, your accusers are attempting to apply reason to a situation where that concept has been hijacked and inverted. They walk away frustrated. You walk to the bar.

*****

In his brilliant piece called "The Five Levels of Drinking," Larry Miller describes the end of an all-nighter in which you and your friends wind up in a neighboring state at nine in the morning drinking a blue liquid served by a barmaid with fresh stitches in her head.

He goes on to say that when you finally open the door to leave "the sun is like God's flashlight." Man, does that resonate with me. Sunday mornings during my partying years frequently found me walking home just before dawn in what I like to describe as a scampering stagger.

There is something about a lengthy drug and alcohol escapade that loves the cover of darkness. Bingeing is inherently a nocturnal activity. The cloak of night allows you to pretend your behavior was harmless and that you look as good as you feel. But the morning sun is the district attorney. He has videotape from the scene of the crime. And he can't wait to see your face when he shows it to the jury.

If you stand on an urban street corner at dawn on Sunday you can hear the sun laughing and taunting the Saturday night drug vampires as it nips at their ankles and chases them home. "Run you little shits, the mighty truth is shining right behind you."

Having once again narrowly escaped the morning light, I would very quietly close the outside door and would find myself standing in the hallway and staring at the door to my apartment. This is a difficult moment to describe. It is a journey deep into a world of overwhelming fear and guilt. But because fear and guilt are under the influence of cocaine and alcohol this morning, they bear very little resemblance to their sober counterparts.

There is a special terror associated with this moment.

The walls are pulsating. I desperately try not to make any noise but with each step the floorboards creak like little screaming demons. I slip in my key with the skill and precision of a cat burglar and slowly, with shaking hands, open the door to the kitchen.

And there she is.

Standing in her nightgown.

The morning sun, unable to shine the light of day upon me as I scampered home moments before dawn, has resourcefully slipped through my kitchen window. A diligent and tenacious nemesis, his failure to accomplish his primary goal of revealing my true identity to the world only steeled his resolve to fulfill his secondary desire. He has placed a stream of warm morning light ever so delicately upon the side of her face and in so doing has visually articulated, with a clarity that language can only dream of, the immensity of the pain that I have caused this woman.

Here in her kitchen on Sunday morning all her humble dreams of a family life where children can grow up in an atmosphere of love and normalcy are in flames. Her eyes stare vacantly at this train wreck she calls her husband while he stumbles past her to collapse on top of their bed.

Later I wake up, still high after spending a couple of

hours with a distant cousin of sleep. I lie there and try to muster the courage to open my eyes. I open them slowly. I move my head one quarter of an inch and a sledgehammer, swung from the hand of a righteous God, lands squarely upon my temple.

*****

Early one Sunday morning I returned home from a concert performance. I closed the outside door behind me and found myself looking at the apartment door. I was immediately overcome with fear and guilt. The walls were pulsating. The ghost of Pavlov was sitting on the stairs, smirking. I had begun the guilty cokehead slow creep toward the apartment door when I realized I was sober. I threw Pavlov out on his pompous ass and kicked the door open like Ralph Cramden. "BABY I'M HOME! IT'S THREE IN THE MORNING AND I AM SOBER!" I wanted her to wake up and do the I'm-a-good-boy-I-don't-have-to-feel-guilty-anymore dance with me. Unfortunately, three o'clock in the morning was not what she considered an appropriate hour for dancing. She said, "You used to be a drunk, inconsiderate asshole, now you just don't drink anymore." I resisted the temptation to say, "One of these days Alice, POW! ZOOM!" and went to bed.

*****

I had been clean and sober for over two years when I decided that it was time to "break out." It was a Friday. The kids were away in Maine for the weekend and my wife was going to be out with her girlfriends. I had one hundred and fifty dollars. All day at work I could feel it in my pocket. It was alive. Drug money actually has a heartbeat. As it got closer to the end of the workday, my heart began racing in anticipation of partying all night with my friends. My mind was filled with the memories of countless escapades from my heyday. The excitement, the camaraderie, the feeling that we were squeezing every ounce of living out of each second—it was all I could think about.

When I got home, the house was empty. The kids were already in Maine and my wife was out for the night. I opened my little address book with the phone numbers of all my drinking pals and I laid it next to the phone. I felt like a kid on Christmas morning. Then, staring at the open book, it occurred to me that all day long my mind had been focusing on the ten percent of my drug and alcohol memories that fell into the victimless fun category. It was deliberately ignoring the other ninety percent of associated memories from that era that nearly cost me everything that I held dear. I thought to myself, "Why is my mind working against me?"

This question triggered an interesting series of events. First I got angry. I kept thinking, "I need my mind to do what is best for me. This is clearly an example where that is not the case." Then I forced myself to call up a random cross section of extremely painful drug and alcohol memories.

Being carried home at four in the morning by my friends and dumped on my kitchen floor.

Puking out the window of my friend's car.

Having no idea where I left my own car and calling a cab in the morning to drive me around town to find it.

Driving home so drunk I could have killed ten people and not remembered.

Random daily nosebleeds.

Spending all night immersed in long, intimate conversations with people that I would normally cross the street to avoid, simply because they had lots of drugs and were willing to share them with me.

The memories were as abundant as they were nauseating. The evidence was overwhelming. This mind could not be trusted. Well, ain't this a dilemma? If a man is deliberately trying to hurt you, you could, in theory, just kill him. But if you are being betrayed by your own mind, applying the same solution poses certain . . . complications. When presented with the statement "My mind is working against me," the only response I could think of was to tear off my own head.

Then I saw the Viking ship. I can still see it.

It is a ship on the ocean. One hundred men row in pairs. This ship is my mind. The ocean is my life. Each pair of rowers represents a piece of the team that is responsible for the health and development of one specific part of who I am. The first two guys are the ones who make sure I get out of bed in the morning and make it to work on time. The next two make sure that I am reasonably honest. The next pair help me to be a good father. And so on. All of these people are doing a fantastic job. They know what their role on the team is and they are focused and determined to do their part to keep this ship moving in the direction of my continued evolution.

In the center of the ship are the two guys who like to party. They are turned around and trying to row in the opposite direction.

As this image took shape between me and my address book, I began to laugh. I thought to myself, "My mind isn't working against me. I just have a couple of bad employees.

I don't need to tear my head off. I just need to discipline these two nitwits, who apparently haven't read their job descriptions."

So I call them into my office. I address them formally. "Mister Nit and Mister Wit. You two are giving the prison work release program a bad name. You see how all the other team members are doing a fantastic job keeping this ship moving forward? If you think for one minute that I am going to sit back and let you little turds undermine the morale of this organization, you must be outcho' fuckin' mind! I'm giving you both a written warning. And, since you are merely figments of my imagination, if you continue with this insubordination, I will feel no obligation to give you a second warning. Figments have no right to due process. Figments have no rights at all. I will simply have you both thrown overboard."

The sun had gone down. The house had grown dark. My heart was no longer racing with anticipation. The money in my pocket had stopped beating. As soon as it learned that it was not going to be drug money, it suffered a massive heart attack and died. I closed my little book of phone numbers and put it away. I sat on the couch and turned on the Celtics game. As I settled into the familiar comfort of my living room, I whispered these words. "Your mind is not working against you. You just have a couple of bad employees. Deal with them."

The Boys Club

Chapter One
The Domain of Anthropology

I am forty-seven. Forty-seven is very old.

Don't argue with me. I'm right about this. Just ask my kids.

The joy that my children acquire from asking me what life was like during the Ice Age hasn't diminished discernibly since they began their irreverent inquiry ten years ago. Even now, after all these years, their question still initiates a dance frenzy among the genes of disrespectful taunting that my wife and I unwittingly passed on to these people.

I still live in the city of my youth. But unlike many American cities, Lynn, Massachusetts has not gone through the wholesale mall-ification that has cemented over the memories of so many of my fellow Americans.

To the casual observer, my neighborhood has been frozen in time. A snapshot taken today from the living room window of the house in which I was raised would look very similar to one taken in 1965.

However, these eyes of mine that now peer out at the world through magnifying glass know very well that, aside from the location of the streets and houses, the world they so clearly observed between 1962 and 1974 has been relegated to the domain of anthropology.

In response to the irreverent inquiries of my incurably disrespectful children—and as a public service to the anthropological community—I am going to try to capture the essence of what it was like to be a child in my neighborhood millions of years ago in the nineteen-sixties.

I'd like to begin with a lexicon of key terms from the lost dialect of my youth:

Dinkweed. A derogatory term for an individual, very similar to asshole. Can also be used as a term of endearment.
Ice bucky. A floating block of ice in the brackish section of the Saugus river.
Jumping buckies. Jumping from one floating ice block to another.
Muckle. A game where the boy with the ball runs for his life while everyone else chases him and attempts to tackle or "muckle" him to the ground.
Polio pool. A public cement swimming pool of the kind once located in the playgrounds.
Sticker bushes. Common burdock.
Whiffle. A crew cut. A very short haircut.

My wife and I have had access to two important things that have enabled us to raise our children in ways that differed dramatically from the methods employed by our parents: tremendous advances in the fields of surveillance and communications technology and, much more importantly, the will to use them.

Our kids never walked anywhere. We drove them to and from school. It didn't matter where they were going. We always drove them there and returned to pick them up, even when they were teenagers.

In light of this fact, it is inconceivable that my children could even begin to comprehend the outrageous amount of unsupervised time that I had as a child. Or the influence that freedom had in shaping my personality.

At the age of nine, before I left my house on Saturday morning, I would tell my mother that I was going to eat lunch at my friend's house. My only responsibility thereafter was to be home at six for supper. This was a world where the thought that your mother could use her super powers to cause a telephone to ring in your pocket whenever she felt like it, would (were we able to even conceive of such a thing) have been the stuff of nightmares.

There was no such thing as a cell phone. There was nobody out looking for us. There were no rules at all except "be home for supper." Every Saturday, and almost every day during the summer, my friends and I would step out into our world and manifest what we called an adventure, but what now looks a lot like a ten-hour crime spree.

Chapter Two
Spank the Baby

There is a set of railroad tracks that cuts through the neighborhoods of West Lynn. These tracks have long been abandoned, but during the Ice Age a freight train would roll past my street almost every day. In the summer, my friends and I would spend the day playing jack-knife games. (I guess you could say that jack knives were the video games of the sixties.) Two kids would sit across from each other on the lawn in the corner of a back yard and go through a predetermined series of methods by which to get the knife to stick into the ground. You would start with just throwing it straight down. Next you would place the point gently on your baby finger and flip it toward the ground. Then you would duplicate this procedure flipping the knife from each finger in turn. In the finale—something called spank the baby—you would hold one hand palm down, slide the blade of the knife under your index finger, over your middle and under your ring finger so that your ring and index fingers were holding the blade on top of your middle finger. Then you would slap the protruding handle with your free hand. If you were successful, the knife would flip into the air and stick in the ground.

Then there was the jack-knife version of chicken—a fabulous way for children to kill time and manufacture scar tissue on one another. Two kids stand opposite each other with their feet apart. One kid throws the knife into the ground between the feet of the other. The second kid, moving one of his feet to where the knife landed so the space between his feet is effectively cut in half, pulls the knife out of the ground and then throws it between the feet of the first kid. This alternating procedure continues until the space between the feet of each participant is so small that one kid either chickens out or gets stabbed in the foot. Serious players often choose the barefoot version.

So, we're playing spank the baby in my back yard when the sound of a freight train turns all of our heads in unison, in exactly the same way that a gunshot would turn all the heads in a herd of deer. Without a word, we jump up and start running toward the tracks.

At the end of my street was an old age housing project. The section of the tracks that ran through my neighborhood was behind these buildings on the other side of a tall picket fence. We all lined up at a hole in the fence that was big enough for an average ten-year-old boy to pass through if he bent down and slid through sideways. The whole process took about one minute but to me it was an eternity. "Hurry up you fat bastid. The train'll be in Chelsea by the time we all get through."

The railroad tracks were like a trail of lawlessness carved through the heart of the city. When I pushed my head through that fence, it was like peeking through a portal into another world. When I slid my eighty-pound body through and was standing in the tall ragweed, it was like running away from home. It was the urban equivalent of being west of the Pecos. ("No *señor*, there is no law west of the Pecos.")

The section of the tracks nearest my house was about as long as a city block. There were probably twenty back yards that abutted this stretch. Fortunately for the delinquent population, many of the abutters had erected tall picket fences to block their view of the activities that took place just beyond their property lines. This was a tremendous help in providing freedom of movement for me and my friends.

Once everyone was on the tracks we all hunkered down in the weeds and waited. Donny Underwood pulled a penny out of his pocket and placed it on the rail. After the steel behemoth had lumbered through our neighborhood, Donny would be the proud owner of a flattened piece of copper. We all had one. It was like a membership card to our secret society.

On this day, however, I was not interested in adding to my mashed coin collection—I had more adventurous intentions.

We could see that the train had stopped at Spencer Street.

Between downtown Lynn and the salt marsh in Saugus, the train had to cross at least seven streets. There were no automated railroad crossings to stop traffic. One of the railroad workers on board would just jump off the train and stand in the middle of the street, holding out his open palms as the train rolled through.

Soon the sound of the engine began to roar again and the train moved slowly toward us. Behind the engine were three tall gray cars full of rock salt, two flat bed cars, and a caboose. It stopped again at Cottage Street. When it started moving this time we all jumped out of the weeds and ran toward it. I had my eye fixed on the third salt car. I preferred the salt cars to the flat cars because they had a small area at each end where you could stand and enjoy the ride while holding one of two vertical poles for balance.

The train began to pick up speed as we ran toward it. I was perhaps eight feet from my car of choice when Ronnie Preston ran past me and jumped up on it leaving me no way on. As the train picked up even more speed I found myself running as fast as I could toward the second flatbed car. It was my only chance to get on because the only car behind it was the caboose, and ever since the Jimmy Spiliotis incident last summer everyone knew to never jump on the caboose.

The deck of a flatbed car is perhaps four or five feet from the ground. To board, a person must use the step and handle that are welded to each car for this express purpose. The handle is made of round metal stock, the diameter of a thin broom handle. It comes straight out about eight inches, bends ninety degrees, extends for a foot and a half, and then bends another ninety degrees back to the frame of the car.

The step is directly beneath the handle. It is made of flat stock. Think of it as a letter U made from eighteen-inch straight lines vertically and horizontally and welded to the bottom of the car's bed. The horizontal section is what you put your feet on. The distance from the handle to the bottom of the step is approximately three feet.

When a train is not moving or moving slowly, all you have to do is grab the handle, put your foot on the step, and either hang there and enjoy the ride or push with your legs as you pull with your hands to get up on to the car.

This endeavor becomes significantly more challenging with each accelerating mile-per-hour.

But I am ten years old and I fear nothing save a life without adventure. I piss in the ear of mortality. "I am jumpin' this train!"

It's a good thing that my mother bought me these P.F. Flyers because the TV commercial says that these sneakers will make you run faster and jump higher. I believe it. I really am running faster!

I grabbed the handle with both hands and jumped. I watched my left foot slip off the step and slide through the center of the U. My whole leg up to the crotch was now underneath the train. My right foot just barely managed to land on the step.

As I tried to reconfigure my body in a way that would allow me to pull my leg out from under the train, I watched the rear metal wheel spin at thirty miles per hour three inches from my left ankle.

I eventually righted myself and pulled my leg back and placed my left foot in the proper place.

When the train stopped to cross Boston Street, my friends jumped off near a bar called the Crystal. They began walking back to the neighborhood. I decided to stay on and ride to Saugus Center. Riding this section of the tracks always gave me the feeling that I was outside the boundaries of the known world. The two miles from the Crystal to Saugus Center is a salt marsh—no houses—so the train really goes fast through there.

I held on, threw my head back, and let the wind hit my face to the screech and roar of metal on metal.

As the train slowed down at the end of the marsh I decided to jump off. I never rode the train past Saugus Center. It seemed so rural there that I wasn't sure if the next stop might be Kansas. It was true that I didn't have to be home for lunch, but even though I had consistently flunked geography in school I was still pretty sure that I couldn't walk all the way home from the Midwest by suppertime.

I jumped off the train while it was still moving and, consistent with the luck this day seemed to have predetermined for me, my feet slipped in some mud and I went tumbling into a patch of ragweed and broken glass. When I stood up and began walking I saw that blood was running down my right forearm from three deep gashes— battle wounds.

As I write this now, I think of myself as an airplane that is circling runway fifty. I have very little in common with this sixth grader, walking alone on the railroad tracks, except that we both love our imaginations and that we both will often prefer time alone with the unlimited possibilities that exist within our respective minds to most social interactions.

We were on patrol. We just survived an enemy ambush. Now I have these three bullet wounds. We have to make it back to our squad before—what's that up ahead? An enemy bunker! I've got this one hand grenade (empty coke bottle) *left. We've got to take 'em out. "Kirby, Little John, cover me." "Don't do it Sarge. It's too dangerous." "Just cover me boys."*

Dash left, dash right, dive behind a boulder. "This is as close as I'm gonna get. If it's not a perfect shot, we're all goners. C'mon baby, the free world is counting on ya. Smooch! Take this you nazi bastards!" (The coke bottle flies through the air, lands on the metal rail and smashes to pieces.) *"He did it! I can't believe it! With three bullet holes in his arm, he threw a perfect strike and saved the whole patrol!"*

—You know, I bet I can walk on the rails without falling off longer than anyone in the world. I must have done it for a mile already. I wonder if wild Indians used to live on this river? I bet they did. They probably paddled their canoes all over this place. OK, there's the Crystal. Watch out for drunks. Jimmy Dyer's dad is always in there. Jimmy and his mother have to go down on Friday and get his paycheck from him before he spends it all. Cool, now we're past Boston Street and back on the tracks again. I think right over there is where those asshole glue-sniffing eighth graders from Woodman Street go buckyin' when the ice starts to melt. Those guys are crazy. Jimmy says he's seen 'em lots a times jumpin' buckies right there near the Crystal. OK, we're getting back near houses now so watch out for enemy patrols. Oh there's that German shepherd—he's mean. I'll put these two rocks in my pockets. If he gets loose from that yard I'll have a second one to aim at his ugly head in case I miss with the first one. I bet Ronnie Estrada's dog Herk could kill that shepherd. Herk is

really tough but he's not mean. He never fights with my dog. My dog
Kipper is little but he's really fast and he is definitely the best jumper.
He can jump a picket fence. I've seen him do it lots of times. Oh shit!
Hear that? Quick—duck behind this rock.

I was on a section of track that runs between two playgrounds. The sound I heard was unmistakable to me. It
was the sound of kids on bikes. This was the summer that
the neighborhood kids figured out how to use clothespins
and baseball cards to give their bikes the sound of a
motor. You use a clothespin to clip the card to the part of
the frame that holds the wheel on to the bike. The card
sticks in between the spokes and makes a thapping sound
as the wheel turns and each spoke hits the card. The
asshole glue-sniffers from Woodman Street all did this.
And there they were riding down the tracks toward me.
Four kids on Stingray bikes. The two in front were
carrying sticker bushes that they had ripped out of the
ground. What we called a "stickah" bush is a plant called
common burdock. It's a bitch of a weed that pops up in
urban areas. At the top of this plant, which can grow four
feet tall, are round balls about as big as a marble. Each ball
is covered with lots of tiny burrs. If you get anywhere near
it, the balls will stick to you. Late in the growing season
they turn brown and break apart easily. Getting them out
of your clothes is a huge pain in the ass because instead of
being able to pick each individual sticker ball off, as soon
as you touch them they break into hundreds of tiny burrs.

Getting them out of your hair is damn near impossible.

I run down in the gully and hide. It's a mess in there—
lots of beer bottles and junk everywhere, plus it's mucky.
My dad told me that Barry Park used to be called Little
River Park because the Saugus River used to run through

some part of it. Well, this must be where it used to run because it's all wet and smelly.

Although these older kids that I was hiding from were always sniffing model airplane glue, their capacity for criminal ingenuity did not seem to suffer as a result. Their ability to utilize the few functioning brain cells that had escaped the ravages of the glue-sniffing life to invent new and exciting methods with which to torment the younger kids in the neighborhood was very impressive indeed. The previous autumn, in a stroke of diabolical genius, they had discovered that common burdock, when pulled from the ground, makes a unique and superb weapon of torture.

They would ride around town looking for someone to attack. Whenever they came across a likely victim (for the record, a skinny sixth grader alone on the railroad tracks is the quintessential "likely victim") they would chase him, knock him down and thrash him with local flora selected specifically for its ability to inflict the kind of suffering that would not only be felt immediately but would increase in the days that followed.

Ragweed when stripped down to the shaft, they had learned, made a fabulous whip. It made an unmistakable and terrifying whishing sound when waved in the air. It would leave a nice welt on the leg of a kid in shorts. The combination of whipping you with ragweed and thrashing you with sticker bushes provided these kids with a double pleasure: the immediate enjoyment derived from delivering your beating, plus the secondary satisfaction of knowing that it would take a week for your welts to heal and for you to get all the sticker balls out of your hair.

Last fall they attacked Ronnie Preston with about four or five stickah bushes. He had so many stickah balls in his hair that his parents had to bring him down to Joe Poof's Barbershop and get him a whiffle. I hate Joe Poof! What kind of name is Poof anyway? S'probably Greek I bet. S'probably shortened from Poofalopapopalous or somethin'. I hate that guy. Last year I told my parents that I did not want a whiffle. I begged Joe Poof not to give me one. I kept telling him that I wanted a Beatle haircut. I wanted to have a piece of hair that hung down over my eyes so I could be cool. Did I get a Beatle haircut? No. That dinkweed gave me a whiffle and he left a little patch in the front that my mother would put brylcream in to make it stand up straight. When I look at my school picture from last year with my big ears hanging off my head and my stupid whiffle with the Joe Poof brylcream patch in the front, I could puke. Whiffles suck. I am NEVER getting another one as long as I live. I'll run away from home first. I'll jump a freight and I won't get off till I'm in California. Jimmy says these tracks go all the way to California.

Debbie Bouley is never gonna go steady with a kid who has a stupid whiffle.

As I hid in the mucky gully, I pulled the two rocks out of my pockets. There was no way that I could avoid getting rat packed, sticker bushed and pummeled by these guys if they saw me, but I had made up my mind to bust open the head of at least one of them before they beat the shit out of me. At least that was what I was thinking. The truth is that I was just talking tough to myself. I knew two things: If they caught me I'd cry like a baby; and these guys were probably so gone on glue that even if I did crack one of their heads open with a rock, he probably wouldn't even know it till tomorrow.

They drove past. They never even looked into the gully. I waited until they had disappeared around the bend toward the river and then I climbed through a hole in the chain link fence and into Barry Park. When the adrenaline that was pumping through my body began to subside, I realized how badly my arm hurt. The three gashes were still bleeding and my fingers were tingling.

Chapter Three
Barry Park 1967

Barry Park was bustling. Everywhere you looked there were groups of kids engaged in various activities. I walked past six boys who were getting ready to play baseball. The three legitimate diamonds were occupied so these guys were going to play on a makeshift diamond that existed in the center of the park. The bases had been created by pulling up grass and leaving patches of dirt. These sandlot style games made up of three person teams had wonderful ground rules.

If you hit the bleachers it's a home run.

If you hit the ball over the bleachers it's a grand slam.

If you hit it over the bleachers and into that crazy guy's yard, it's still a grand slam but you gotta go get the ball yourself.

You can only hit to one field. Balls hit to center and the opposite field are foul.

When your team is hitting, one of your guys has to be the catcher and if there's a play at the plate he can't pretend to drop the ball.

If two of your guys get on base, one of them has to become the catcher and will be replaced on base by an invisible man. (This rule would often lead to fights over whether an invisible man could have scored from second on a single to left field. "Our invisible man is Rico Petrocelli. He coulda scored from first on that play." "Shit no! Your invisible man is George Scott and he's still tryin' to drag his big butt to third.")

And if the teenagers want to play, they have to hit opposite-handed.

In the business of picking sides for a team that will consist of only three players, the importance of picking first cannot be overemphasized. The team that has to pick second is usually in for a long afternoon of losing. So, over many decades a sophisticated procedure was developed to ensure that this important decision would be determined in a way that could be won by anyone, regardless of age, size, baseball prowess, or current social status within the group.

I sat and watched the familiar ritual while three red rivers rolled down my arm creating little blood ponds on the bleachers.

This is hard to describe, so pay attention.

The duly elected representative of Team One, Joey, took a bat and held it upside down. He then declared the rules by saying, "no topsies, no helicopters." He threw the bat to his counterpart, Billy, who snagged it in mid-flight with his right hand. With the bat held upside down between them, Joey carefully studied the distance between his opponent's hand and the knob at the base of the bat. In order to pick first you need to be the person with his fist or fingers pressed between the fingers of your opponent and the knob. (Are you still with me?) Joey wrapped his fist around the bat just above Billy's fist. There was not enough room to fit another fist between Joey's hand and the knob so Billy did the only other thing that the rules allowed. He opened his index and middle finger and slid them around the bat handle above Joey's fist. Joey did the same thing, leaving just enough space for Billy to do it once more. This filled the remaining space between the knob of the bat and Joey's fingers and gave Billy "first pick."

Had Joey not initially proclaimed "no topsies" the rules would have allowed him to place the palm of his free hand on top of the inverted bat. However, if helicopters were not excluded Billy would have then held his index and middle finger over the bat and wiggled them up and down for victory.

Billy immediately picked the one remaining big kid for his side and, I assumed, guaranteed his team an afternoon of consecutive victories—the speed of invisible men notwithstanding.

The bleachers in Barry Park are made of cement. They extend the entire length of one side of the park. I walked on them past some girls who were jumping rope. Two other girls stood nearby facing each other and playing some kind of hand jive game. As they sang this song they would snap their fingers, slap their right hip, clap their hands, touch right hands, clap, touch left hands, clap, and touch both hands twice before starting over again with a finger snap.

Eenee meenie tootsaleenie
You are thumbalini
Aah-cha gaah-cha liberaah-cha
C O D

Take a peach. Take a plum.
Take a stick of bubble gum.
Not a peach. Not a plum.

Not a stick of bubble gum.

Hey teacher Dum de dum
Gimme back my bubble gum
Hey boy, what's your name?
Joey—greetings—hot dog
Gimme some
Jump out the window
Singing,

Eenee meenie tootsaleenie
You are thumbalini
Aah-cha gaah-cha liberaah-cha
C O D

Every activity in the park had its own unique music. The girls jumping rope were actually singing songs but even a kid hollering information to his teammates from left field seemed to have more than a hint of the town crier in his voice. "Two outs, man on third, invisible man on secoonndd." "Allee, allee, in-come-freeee." "Red rover, red rover, send Jimmy right over."

Across the street I saw a boy standing on the steps of his friend's house. He rolled his head back and began singing his friend's name: Tawm-eeee, Tawm-eeee. We never rang doorbells or knocked on doors. We just stood on your porch and sang your name until you came out or your mom chased us away.

From behind me on Waterford Street I heard a song that was new to me. I turned around and saw two older kids who lived way down by the West Lynn General Electric factory. They looked like they were drunk. They were leaning shoulder to shoulder on each other as they walked down the middle of the street in what seemed like an imitation of the way the mummy walked in the horror movies—leaning slightly back and moving each leg as if it had no bendable knee. Their song came to my ear and for some reason has stayed there ever since.

Greasy, grimy gopher's guts
Chocolate covered birdie's feet
Rollin' down the bloody street
And me without my spoon.

There was great sadness in their voices as they sang the last line. I could feel the deep sense of opportunity lost that they were experiencing at having found themselves spoonless in the presence of such a magnificent feast.

After they had harmonized their way past me and mummy-walked over toward the polio pool, I climbed down from the bleachers. I walked across Cottage Street to Waterhill Street. With a new song of opportunity lost on my lips—and keeping a sharp eye out for jerks on stingrays—I headed home.

I was putting my key in the back door when Mrs. Nicholson called my name from the fence that separated our yard from hers. "What happened to your arm?" I said that I cut it while sliding into second base. Her eyes made note of the fact that I was not carrying a baseball glove and then flashed me the I-know-you're-lying look. I acknowledged it and ignored it.

No one over the age of twelve ever heard anything resembling the truth from me in those days. I even lied to adults on those rare occasions when I was innocent and was in possession of a legitimate alibi. It was just easier for me to remember to never tell them the truth than to try to determine in which situations the truth might prove advantageous.

Mrs. Nicholson told me that my parents were out. She made me walk around to her front door and brought me into her kitchen. She washed off my wounds, covered them in iodine and put band-aids on them. While she was finishing the job I glanced up at her face. I didn't have the wherewithal or the inclination to interpret what her face was saying at the time. But the look she gave me has never faded from my memory. As I reflect upon it now, I know exactly what it was saying: "This poor child will never live to see twenty."

Chapter Four
The Boys Club

There was a knock at the door while we were having dinner that evening. My mother answered it. It was Ronnie Preston. He said that his phone was broken and asked if he could use ours. Our phone was in the kitchen so we all heard his conversation. "Hello, my dad is drunk and he's bustin' up the house. He ripped the phone off the wall. No, I'm at a neighbor's house. That's right, send a cruiser and get him out of there." He gave the address, hung up the phone, thanked my mother and left. We all sat at the table and continued to eat our American chop suey. No one spoke.

After dinner my brother got in the front seat of my dad's gigantic white Chrysler. I got in the back. Some time in the seventies, automobile makers stopped designing back seats with comfortable sex in mind. Not so with dad's Chrysler. You could have put a trampoline back there.

It was my father's turn to drive the local hoodlums to the Boys Club. He drove around the neighborhood, pulled up in front of each kid's house and tooted the horn. One by one my friends came out of their houses and climbed into the Chrysler. The last kid that we picked up that night was Ronnie Preston.

When my Dad dropped us off that evening, Ronnie pulled me aside and said, "I suppose everyone knows about what happened tonight." I didn't know how to respond. He was apparently under the impression that the drunk dad thing was something that I would be anxious to tell everyone about. He was obviously unaware of the fact that good fortune had arranged a situation in which the neighbors closest to his house, from whom he could request the use of a telephone, had a deep and long-standing familiarity with the drunk dad experience. As far as I knew, everyone had a drunk dad. I didn't know there was any other kind. It never occurred to me to mention anything about it to anyone. It wasn't a thinking thing. I just grew up knowing not to talk about it.

*****

The Boys Club is still in the same brick building on North Common Street next to the public library. Today it is called the Boys and Girls Club—an absolutely inconceivable notion in 1967. "Girls? Are you kidding? What the hell would a girl do at the Boys Club? What are they gonna do next, let boys into the Girls Club?"

I have no idea what goes on in that building now but in

1967 it was a club for boys. The front door opened into a big
room. There were some bumper pool tables over to the left.
The room directly to the right as you entered had a black-
and-white TV and some chairs in case boys wanted to relax
in front of the tube. The room next to that had two ping
pong tables.

If you turned left as soon as you came in the front
door you would pass the office and arrive at a stairwell. At
the base of those stairs was a candlepin bowling alley—
two or three lanes. No automation whatsoever. After you
rolled your three balls down the lane a boy would climb
down from a cubbyhole above the pins. He would roll
your balls back to you on the wooden rail, reset the pins
by hand, and disappear. This was a highly coveted job
because it paid something like ten cents a string. The Boys
Club bowling alley was designed so that even after the
Russians (remember the Russians? They were the political
equivalent of today's Muslim terrorists) had bombed out
our electrical power plants, Americans would still be able
to go bowling.

At the top of those stairs on the second floor was a big
room that held several regulation size pool tables—the
kind with the leather pockets. This room had the same
ambiance as a downtown pool hall minus the whiskey and
cigarette smoke.

Most of the activities that took place in the Boys Club
were directed toward, well, boys. Not so with this room.
To me it seemed like a section of the building for grown-
ups—a Mens Club, if you will.

I would sometimes stand just inside the door and take
in the sights and sounds of this room. I watched older,
tough-looking teenagers as they leaned on pool cues and

studied the configuration of balls on the table, each boy oblivious to the sad irony proclaimed by his F in geometry as he silently reveled in his mastery of this game.

I listened intently as tales of great criminal adventures were told with captivating street-savvy eloquence. The strategic curse words that these young men included in their storytelling never seemed to be forced or inappropriate. In fact, their use of profanity had a natural ease of which I was quite envious.

The rear of the building housed an Olympic swimming pool. At the very end of the building was a gym with basketball courts and a small track. There was also a boxing ring back there where, under adult supervision, boys could beat the shit out of each other.

In the minds of our parents the Boys Club did two things: combat juvenile delinquency and keep young men off the street. Once I stop laughing, I'll tell you what I think about this.

OK. I have never in my life seen more bona fide juvenile delinquents in one building than I saw during my membership years at the Boys Club. The idea of plunking an impressionable ten-year-old into this cast of characters and expecting him not to acquire the walk, talk, attitude, and skills of a delinquent is absurd beyond description. And as far as keeping kids off the street—Puh-leeeze.

Our parents allowed my brother and I to play outside after dark as long as we stayed within earshot of the house. But on the nights when we went to the Boys Club we would sign in at the side door, walk directly to the front door, and leave the building. To do what, you ask? Why, to run wild on the streets and engage in juvenile delinquency, of course.

On the night of my awkward drunk dad conversation with Ron, we entered the building, signed in, and made plans. "Let's go to the second swim and then play muckle out on the Common after."

The three designated pool usage times on Friday and Saturday nights were called first swim, second swim, and third swim. Our group preferred the second swim because it would be dark outside when it was over. The activities that we participated in outside the building between the end of the second swim and the arrival of our ride home at ten o'clock were specifically designed to take place under cover of darkness.

After signing in we all went in different directions. I immediately left the building and walked down North Common Street to Harvey's Drug Store to work on my shoplifting skills.

Harvey's was smaller than most of the other drug stores in the city—no soda fountain, just a narrow store with a cash register a few feet in from the door on the left and a pharmacy counter at the back. I was the only "customer" this night. I walked directly to the scene of the impending crime as the woman at the counter and the pharmacist both stared at me. I pretended they were too stupid to see me. I bent down at the candy rack, picked up two Oh Henry candy bars, stuck one into my pants, and walked to the counter to pay for the other one.

The most striking thing I remember about this part of my life is the reckless abandon with which I walked through my world.

The head I carry on my shoulders today is entirely incapable of understanding the thinking that took place (or did not take place) inside the head upon my shoulders in Harvey's Drug Store in 1967.

If I use my 2005 brain to contemplate stealing a candy bar from a store, my forty-seven years of life experience will be built into the decision making process. First there will be an internal debate on the subject of gain versus risk.

Why do I need to steal a candy bar? I can afford to buy it. The guy who owns the store is just trying to make a living. What if I get caught? How do I explain it to my wife and kids? This is stupid. I don't even like candy.

Forty-seven years add a lot of perspective.

OK, so don't shoplift, just think about how you would do it if you weren't such an upstanding citizen.

Well, I'd shave, comb my hair and dress in a suit. I'd have an unshaven, twentyish male, preferably Black or Hispanic and dressed in a baggy hooded sweatshirt, go in before me. I'd instruct him to pick expensive things off the shelves and act suspiciously in the way that street punks do on television. While my partner was exploiting the community's prevailing racism and social stereotyping, I would casually fill my suit pockets with enough Oh Henry candy bars to satisfy my sweet tooth and those of my friends for a week.

This is how my grown-up mind works. It's logical. It sizes up the situation and puts together some kind of a plan. It takes into consideration the way in which people in a given community are likely to view the world and then tries to exploit those tendencies.

There was no such activity inside my head in 1967. No plan, no logic, and certainly no big view of the world. This is what I was thinking as I walked to the drug store.

As soon as Jimmy Spiliotis jumped on that caboose last summer, the door opened up and out came an engineer. He poured a whole bucket of water on Jimmy who fell off the train and lay there on his ass all soakin' wet while we all rode to Saugus laughing our heads off. OK here's Harvey's. Candy bar? Sure, no problem.

Upon reflection, I think that in 1967 I just didn't comprehend the idea of going into a store without shoplifting.

I could tell by the look on the face of the woman at the counter and by the sound of the approaching footsteps of the pharmacist (perhaps Harvey himself) that they were on to the candy bar caper. I ran out the door, turned left into the high school yard, and ran around behind the building. I quickly climbed over a couple of chain link fences behind the apartment buildings that stand between the school and the Boys Club and then casually walked in the side door with a new story to tell at the second swim.

Chapter Five
Second Swim 1967

First a short digression.

The world that I am writing from today has a lot of fear in it. It's mostly because of television. Television is a soul-crushing diabolical motherfucker determined to suck the joy of living out of mankind. Television—and especially television news—needs to be taken out behind the barn and beaten to within an inch of its life.

In my day when parents would spank their kids they would simultaneously threaten them. These threats were spoken one syllable at a time, each syllable coinciding with each open-handed blow to your bottom.

"If I e ver catch you on those god damn trains a gain I will beat you to with in an inch of your life young man!"

Picture me dragging television out behind the barn and saying this as I give him the spanking he deserves.

"If I e ver catch you dri ving past four teen mil yun nice pee ple to find one ba by rape ing ass hole in Kan sas that you can talk a bout twen ty four se ven to de lib er ate ly strike fear in to the hearts of ev ry one by im ply ing that ev ry third house has a pe do phi le in it so they will fear the world out side and stay home and watch T V all day while pur chas ing pro ducts from your spon sors by phone, I will beat you to with in a min ute of your planned ob so les cence!!!"

I graduated from high school in the spring of 1974. During that summer I decided I was going to leave Lynn before winter and hitchhike around the country. Everyone thought I was nuts. This was before cable TV, cell phones, and the disproportionate fear of all things, but still no one was on board for the hitchhiking idea.

A week before I was to leave, I ran into a friend of mine on Western Avenue. He asked me, "Aren't you afraid of what might happen to you out there?"

I was seventeen years old. He and I were standing in front of a bar called the 757. Directly across the street was a bar called Burke's. When I say bars, I mean little hole-in-the-wall places where it was not uncommon to see two drunks come crashing out the front door and into the street beating the hell out of each other. Just to the left of Burke's was a pizza place called Caruso's. As my friend was asking this question, I was recalling a day when I made the unfortunate and unforgivable mistake of saying hello to some jerk's girlfriend in there. Two minutes later I was getting my head kicked in on the sidewalk in front of

Caruso's while my chickenshit friends sped off on their bikes. I was ten years old.

I responded to my friend's question by asking, "What the hell am I going to bump into out there that could possibly be more fucked up than this place?" Then I swung my arms and encouraged him to take a good hard look at the West Lynn of our day.

Look, I had no idea what I was talking about. Maybe Lynn was a friendlier place than the rest of the country. Maybe the ass-kickings that I would receive out there would cause me to long nostalgically for the relatively tame thumpings of my youth. Maybe someone would kill me. I didn't know. I was guessing.

Looking back now though, I can see I was right. Between November 1974 and November 1979 I spent a total of thirty months with my thumb out on the highways of the U.S. and Canada. Most of that time I was with my future wife. Every single day we met people who had the opportunity to do us harm—thousands of them from every corner of the continent. Not once did anyone lay a hand on either of us. To the complete bewilderment of every person with a television in America, I say that during nearly three years of hitchhiking, we were the constant recipients of tremendous kindness and generosity from strangers.

Television doesn't create murderers and rapists. It creates the misconception that they are everywhere.

When someone tells me that the world used to be a safer place, the term "thinning out the herd" comes to my mind. I can't help but think about the animal kingdom and how the slow elk are routinely killed by wolves, thereby ensuring that only the smart and swift will reproduce.

The world was not safer. The world was stupider. It was

stupid for ten-year-olds to go all day without supervision. It is equally stupid to believe that the percentage of people in society that are spending each waking moment looking for a stranger to hurt is a million times higher in 2005 than it was in 1967.

1967 stupid was the product of naiveté.

2005 stupid is the product of corporate-sponsored, ratings-driven, cynical, self-serving manipulation.

*****

As we lined up for the second swim I was telling my friends about my adventure at Harvey's and the chase scene that followed. In the hour between the incident and the telling of the story I had taken several substantial liberties with the truth, embellishing the tale with the addition of police cars, searchlights, and a physical confrontation with Harvey himself.

As soon as we checked in to the second swim we all went to the locker room. We sat on the flat, backless benches. Each of us placed our clothes in a locker. Then we walked to the pool. I don't know how many kids were allowed at each swim—fifty, a hundred? I do know two things: there were lots of boys there, and they were all naked.

I began this story by saying that I know that I am old. Allow me to nail the door shut on that proclamation.

As a child I went swimming with a hundred naked boys—most of whom were strangers to me—every weekend. Trying to reconcile that memory with the world from which I am writing today makes me feel like Methuselah.

How much media coverage do you think a story about

naked swimming at the Boys Club would generate today? It'd be bigger than the O.J. Simpson case. Pravda would devote twenty hours a day to it. (Did I just say Pravda? I meant to say the Fox News Network. Sorry.)

But less than forty years ago it was the norm.

1967: "Hey Mom everyone swims naked at the Boys Club. Can I join and swim naked too?" "Sure. The Boys Club combats juvenile delinquency."

2005: "Hey Mom can I walk next door to play with Tommy?" "No. Get your cell phone. I'll drive you there and pick you up in an hour. But first I need to get online and do a background check on Tommy's parents."

So there we were every Friday and Saturday night— dozens of prepubescent boys runnin' and a-jumpin', splishin' and a-splashin' with our little wee-wees flippity flopping all over the place. We were the ultimate wet dream of every pedophile that ever lived.

The dance of the boy nymphs was supervised by a fat guy named Bob—ostensibly, to make sure no one drowned. He sat in a lawn chair with an unlit cigar in his mouth and oversaw the proceedings.

For the record, I was never touched or even talked to in a suggestive manner by anyone, young or old, at the Boys Club. Nor did I ever hear tell of anything of that nature ever happening to anyone. I cannot recall one time when the subject ever even came up in conversation. As far as I know, Bob and all the other adults at the Boys Club were, despite their unwillingness to encourage the donning of swimwear and their inability to keep us from leaving the building, good upstanding Americans with high morals and the utmost concern for the welfare of the children in their charge.

Having said that, one can hardly help but wonder if among the pedophiles of the world there has ever been a more enviable job description than Supervisor of the Boys Club Naked Swim. It seems certain that anyone with that job title would be a highly sought-after keynote speaker for the annual pedophile convention.

*****

After the swim my friends and I went outside. We decided not to play muckle on the Common. Instead we played a game of tag on the public library. Yes, I said *on* the library. The outside of that building has numerous places where a person can place their feet and hands for easy scaling. Up at window level there are ledges where you can walk. There are gigantic pillars to hide behind and steps to run up and down upon. This building seems to have been designed specifically for the game of tag. If you drove down North Common Street that night you would have seen a dozen kids climbing up the side of the building, walking along the ledges and jumping from various sections onto the front lawn. It would have looked like a military training course for children.

The air outside the Boys Club during the time between the end of the second swim and ten o'clock was magical and delicious. It was the kind of air that got inside your body and made you believe you could fly. I would fill my lungs with it from atop the window ledge of the library and let it explode out of me with a howl as I jumped off, flew through the air, hit the grass and rolled over and over laughing the laugh of my youth.

Just before ten o'clock we gathered on the front steps

of the Boys Club as if we had just been let out of the building. Dozens of boys from all over the city waited there for their rides home. In the winter this wait would often turn into the artillery target practice portion of our military training. Sometimes upwards of forty delinquent young men would simultaneously throw snowballs at one car. The sound of forty snowballs hitting your car while you are in it is unlike any other motoring experience you are ever likely to encounter. Often the car that we targeted would sway left and right and then pull over. The driver would get out, look across the street at the future inhabitants of the Massachusetts state prison system, and just get back in the car and drive away.

But this was an early autumn night. The air was warm and delicious. We were taunting Jimmy Spiliotis. "How you gonna tell your mom that you didn't leave the building tonight when she sees all those grass stains on your pants? Oh man, you're so busted. Looks like we'll be hoppin' trains without you for a couple of weeks."

Some kids behind us were passing around a cigarette.

It smelled like freedom.

The Dinner Meeting

The Crime

I was walking down Tower Hill one sunny afternoon in 1980 when out of the corner of my eye I saw a green sedan drive past. It was the same color as a car that was owned at the time by someone that I hated—a Mister Kevin Blakeley. Two years earlier he had said and done some things, prior to and during the weekend of my wedding, that infuriated me. I chose to refrain from telling him how I felt at the time, because I didn't want to sour what was otherwise a magical experience. But for the two years since the wedding I had harbored tremendous hatred for him.

He owned a green station wagon. The car that passed me on Tower Hill was a small sedan. The two vehicles were only similar in color but that was enough to bring to the surface of my mind all my unresolved issues with him. As I walked down the street, I initiated an imaginary confrontation. "You miserable, arrogant piece of shit. Who the fuck do you think you are? If you don't like the way I choose to live my life, do us both a favor and stay the hell out of it." My face was contorted. My anger was immense. I'm sure that my lips were moving in a way that made me look like a man in desperate need of a change in medication.

I was just about to take my imaginary club and hit him in the head with it, when I looked up and saw my friend Richard. He was staring at me as if I had gone completely over the edge. "Are you OK?" he asked. It took me a second to de-hatred my mind, but after an awkward pause, I said, "Yeah, I'm fine, I was just thinking about someone who pissed me off." He gave me a look that said, "You should really get some help." And then he walked away.

*****

One warm summer evening in 1995, I was working at the computer in a bedroom on the second floor of my house, when my wife called my name. At that time we were both thirty-eight years old and had been together for twenty years.

Two people who have lived together for more than half their lives have certain modes of communication that are incomprehensible to the rest of the world. For example, it is common knowledge that many qualified members of this segment of society (the severely married) are capable of having entire twenty-minute arguments with their partners telepathically. Mrs. Severely Married will just look at this person with whom she has spent her entire adult life and in a few seconds be able to communicate, with subtle body language and almost imperceptible facial expressions, her side of the argument. And Mr. Married will respond accordingly. It is an extremely effective energy conservation program. And a survival skill.

My wife is particularly masterful at this style of communication. When she crosses her arms and leans her body slightly to one side, I know that is shorthand for her ten-minute diatribe about what an asshole I am for not doing more to help her around the house. When she tilts her head to the right and raises her left eyebrow, that, I know, is shorthand for her brilliant ten-minute indignant response to my feeble attempt to justify my lack of productivity on the weekend with some lame argument about how hard I work during the week. And when she places her hands on her hips and I see heat begin to rise from her head and shoulders, that is her way of telling me in no uncertain terms that I cannot possibly win this argument, and that it is in my best interest to shut the ball game off and help her.

These are twenty-minute, high-volume arguments, done silently in thirty seconds.

In addition to this complex visual language, there is also an entire audio vocabulary between long-time companions through which they can communicate, not so much with words, but by inflection.

My first exposure to this audio phenomenon occurred when my son was an infant. When he wasn't sleeping or staring into the fifth dimension, he was crying. That's what he did, he cried. To me it all sounded the same. One annoying baby sound—waaaaaaaah. However, his mother heard an elaborate, articulate vocabulary within the subtle (and to me imperceptible) differences in every sound that came out of his little mouth. She was equipped with a specialized hearing system that instantly decoded the secret world of infant cryspeak.

Often he would cry in the middle of the night. Sometimes she would ignore him and he would go back to sleep. That waaaaah, she knew, said, "Where the hell am I? Oh, there's my mobile. I know this place. Everything is cool, back to dreamland." Other times she would get up casually and nurse him. She had translated that cry: "I'm starving here. Where's the nice lady with the big tits?"

But occasionally my wife and I would be asleep and our son would begin to cry. Not even a full waaaaaah but just the first waa . . . and she would catapult out of bed and be at that baby's side in two one-hundredths of a second. She knew by the inflection of this sound that he was hurt. He wasn't hungry. He wasn't teething. He wasn't scared. He was in pain and all he had to do was make the "I'm in pain" sound for one millisecond and his mother would instantly appear to untangle his leg from the bars of his crib.

At my computer, my wife's voice penetrated my airspace. One word—two syllables—my name—Donnie. I have heard my wife speak my name nearly every day of my adult life. At last count, she could say it with over four hundred inflections, each clearly communicating a unique reason, motivation, and sense of urgency. From the lips of my wife, my name is an entire language, one that we both speak fluently.

When the first consonant of the first syllable of my name reached my ears it did not make the lengthy trip to my brain for analysis and interpretation. It was snagged and identified by a visceral, adrenaline-driven, high-speed processor located in the pit of my stomach.

This astounding piece of equipment was developed, and used on a daily basis, by prehistoric man in an era when taking the time to think, "Hmm, that sounds like a lion," was more than enough to significantly increase the likelihood of a Cro-Magnon's abrupt and unceremonious return into the food chain.

Move and live. Or think and die.

I move. I do not get up from the chair and run downstairs. I just appear there. My son and his friend are standing in the living room with my wife. They are drenched in trauma. Before a word is spoken I already know that our lives have been permanently altered.

I am now embarking on my sixth attempt at writing this part of the story. On each previous try my mind has acted like a dog being dragged to the veterinarian's office. I know my dog loves me but he hates revisiting this experience so vehemently that he is giving serious thought to biting me in the crotch for forcing him to do it. (I wonder if this is the first time in the history of literature that a reader has been exposed to the possibility of a man being bitten in the crotch by his own mind?)

Anyway.

My son and his friend had just left the variety store around the corner from our house when two junkies accosted them. One of them pressed a pistol against my son's head and took his wallet.

As they told the story I thought about the day my son was born. How beautiful he was. What a wonderful little boy he had been. How excited he and his sister used to get when I came home from work. I remembered them running to meet me at the car as if I had just returned from war. "Daddy's home! Daddy's home!"

When someone I love is in pain I always wish I could shrink them down to about twenty-four inches so I could envelop their entire body and hold their head against my heart. I want my every heartbeat to pulsate through their body and mind with the steady, unwavering, eternal song of my love for them. If my heartbeat had lyrics they would be, "You are safe here."

Prior to this moment I truly believed that the feelings I harbored for Kevin Blakely concerning his behavior at my wedding qualified as hatred. I was wrong. I didn't hate him. I was aggravated with him. I would have been happy just to tell him off. That is not hatred.

Let me tell you what hatred is.

In the hours that followed my son's arrival back home from the mugging we talked to each other and to our ward councilor. We rode around the city with two police officers. We filled out forms at the police station and did many other things. I was on automatic pilot the entire time. I answered questions. I filled out forms. I comforted my son. I did all these things using less than one percent of my attention. The other 99 percent was transfixed on a scene in my mind. In the scene I am standing over this mugger. He is on his back on the sidewalk. I have my foot on his neck. I have a pistol gripped firmly in my right hand. I am looking him in the eye.

And I am blowing his fucking brains out.

As I mechanically go through the motions of being present on earth, I obsessively rerun this scene in my mind and each time as I watch the blood and brains pour out of his miserable head, I feel better and better.

Now that is hatred.

One of the major problems with hatred is that it feels so good. The feelings I was having as I envisioned myself killing this man who was one shaky finger movement away from putting a bullet into the brain of my beautiful son were damn near orgasmic.

Hatred is like heroin. It keeps you on the verge of orgasm as it destroys you.

This brings us back to Tower Hill, with Mr. Kevin Blakeley and the anger that I harbored for him. The first thing I need to acknowledge is that it felt great. I loved hating him. There is something life-affirming about the boiling up of righteous indignation that hatred, triggered by something as transient as the sight of a green car, releases. It is really quite intoxicating.

If the job of a good intoxicant is to remove the person who consumes it from reality, then hatred qualifies as one of the strongest. Drugs seduce you away from your life. It doesn't matter what they offer you as an alternative. Euphoria, sedation, righteous indignation, or delicious hatred are all equally capable of getting the job done.

Spending your precious and irreplaceable time allotment in any of these states of altered consciousness would be perfectly justifiable if you were living in the seventh circle of Dante's Hell. However, if you are not living in a torture chamber, all the moments, hours, days, weeks or decades that you choose to be absent from your life will turn out to be time that did not produce any jewels of kindness or compassion for you to treasure in your old age.

My Nursing Home Education

When I was in my early twenties I worked as a custodian in a nursing home in Waldoboro, Maine. I would mop the floors, paint the rooms, conduct fire alarms and empty the trash. I was paid three dollars and fifteen cents an hour.

This was, coincidentally, the approximate price of a six-pack of Molson ale. I stayed at this job for over a year. I justified it by telling myself that I wasn't really working for twenty-six dollars a day. Each and every day of my gainful employment was earning me eight six-packs of imported ale.

When a person builds an elaborate mental fabrication to justify staying at a job that practically guarantees a future of abject poverty, that person's job performance will quite often suffer from a motivational malaise.

I fucked off a lot.

I had a little room with some tools in it where I would often hide and write songs. Another of my favorite non-custodial activities was talking with the residents. They fascinated me.

A lot of the situations I encountered there were, as you might expect, really sad. There were the Alzheimer's patients whose minds had betrayed them and disconnected them from their life's experiences.

There were the incontinent old men standing against the wall, stinking up the hallway. These guys were in hell. Their eyes revealed a sense of humiliation that was absolute, as absolute as their envy of the Alzheimer's patients.

As I passed one of these men on my rounds one day he asked me, "What tremendous evil did I commit that caused God to curse me at the end of my life with weak plumbing and a strong mind? If God loves you he lets you go out like *that*." He pointed across the hall to a resident with severe Alzheimer's who was drooling out of the side of his mouth and speaking Martian. "If he hates you, he makes you shit yourself twice a day and leaves your mind as sharp as a tack so you can fully experience, for every damn day of your life, the humiliation of having a girl younger than your granddaughter wipe your ass."

There was a relentless cacophony of moaning and complaining. I witnessed episodes where four staff members would carry a screaming octogenarian into the room with the bathtub for a half-hour of forced bathing. (I guess you could call it a gang bath.) And of course, there were the frequent, unannounced visits to our little community by a Mr. Grim Reaper.

But I also witnessed, and participated in, situations that were extraordinarily uplifting, educational, life-affirming, and very funny.

Unlike any other job experience I have had, this one bequeathed several memories that have withstood the test of time. Take, for example, this pre-viagra early morning conversation that I had the unique privilege of sharing with two of my favorite dirty old men.

Dirty Old Man #1 (addressing Dirty Old Man #2, laughing): Even if it was true, which it ain't, what the hell would you do with it, stick it in your mashed potatoes? Hey Junior, come over here a second.

Don: What's up men?

DOM#1: This lying old sack of shit here says he woke up today with a hard-on. He wants you to ask Nurse Williams if we could get everyone together for a little cake and ice cream to celebrate.

DOM#2: That's right! I finally had one of them religious experiences that that preacher is always talking about on Sunday. My weener is born again!

Don: Congratulations, Mr. Simmons. I'm real happy for you.

(DOM#2 makes a move as if he is going to show us

his new trophy.)

Don: Whoa! I believe you. You do not have to point it at me.

DOM#2: Don't worry kid, it's not loaded.

(They both laugh.)

DOM #1: I know what you have there Charlie, that's a piss hard-on. As soon as you piss it'll turn back into that same old oyster you've had down there since 1953. (They are both laughing like two naughty little boys.) Junior, do you know what George Burns said about having sex after sixty-five?

Don: No, and I'm pretty sure that I would rather not know.

DOM#1: He said it was like trying to stick an oyster into a slot machine.

(They are laughing so hard that there are tears in their eyes. I'm thinking that this might be heart attack territory.)

DOM#2: Hey junior, wheel me down to the supply room where they keep all the paint cans and brushes.

Don: What do you want from down there?

DOM#2: I'm gonna shellac this thing before I go to the bathroom.

*****

One of the residents was named Mary. She was totally unresponsive. She never seemed to process a single word that anyone said to her. I never heard her speak. Once or twice a day she would be attacked by an imaginary pack of wolves, or a knife-wielding gang of old-lady-raping motorcycle enthusiasts, or (most frightening of all) a hundred liberal Democrats with voter registration forms.

Mid-coastal Maine was a very conservative place in the seventies. I believe it is fair to assume that the threat of a liberal Democrat invasion and the prospect of being eaten alive by wolves struck an equal degree of fear into the hearts of a lot of the locals.

During the times when Mary was experiencing one of her imaginary dismemberments, gang bangs, or forced registrations, she would open her mouth and let out the most bloodcurdling sound ever to violate the ear of man. It was the sound a woman might make if a rat climbed up her asshole. The first time I heard it, it nailed me to the wall of my workshop and gave me nightmares for weeks.

The word "surreal" is woefully inadequate to describe a nursing home scene where the staff casually go about their business, talking, laughing, filling out paperwork, handing out medication, and answering the phone, to the sounds of an old woman being eaten alive by a pack of wolves.

Reverend James

On Sunday mornings a priest, reverend, or pastor representing one of the local congregations would perform a church service for the residents in the function room.

These guys only came in two flavors. Most common was the bible-thumping, fire-and-brimstone type like Reverend James. What a prick he was. He was from down South somewhere—Virginia I think. He was fresh out of one of those Southern Baptist Bible schools where they teach you all the little tricks you'll need to go out into the world and manipulate the uneducated and emotionally distraught into joining the fold.

When he moved to Maine he hit the motherlode. I always thought of him as a better-dressed version of one of those guys who deal three-card-monte on the sidewalk in Harvard Square.

The church service was merely a vehicle to get him into the building. He would blow through it as quickly as possible and then get to the thing that he really came to do—recruit the staff. He was always trying to get the employees to talk about their problems. I imagine that on day one at the proselytizer manufacturing plant they gave him the secret formula for creating a lifelong member of his future congregation.

"We start with one simple, indisputable fact—Jesus is the answer to all problems. When you graduate you will be a certified representative and authorized spokesperson for him. The only thing that will ever stand between you and bringing one of his stray sheep into your flock is the fact that you don't know what that person's particular problem is." (Don would add to this list of possible obstructions: half a brain, a sense of dignity, a supportive family, or the ability to know a scam artist when you see one.) "Once you get them to tell you their problem, you are well on the way to getting them to join your congregation. Because the answer to their problem, whatever it may be, is Jesus, and Jesus just happens to be the guest of honor at your church every Sunday."

The day I found myself in his Baptist crosshairs was the first time in my life that I began to truly appreciate the fact that I had been raised in an urban community full of hustlers and con artists.

He spotted me in the hallway. I was putting away my mop and bucket and getting ready to knock off for lunch.

He said, "Could I talk to you for a moment, Don?" That's the first trick—they always learn your name and use it frequently in conversation. It is very disarming and even if you know it's a tool, it still makes you feel good. You see politicians do this all the time. "I understand what you are saying, Morton, but I respectfully disagree with you. I feel, much the same as my colleague Congressman Dingus here, that your view is untenable."

He put his arm around my shoulders and walked me a few steps down the hall to the function room. He was much taller than I was so this had the look of a father and son moment.

He suggested that we both sit down. We did. Five seconds later, in a classic strategic maneuver, he stood up. This aggravated me so I stood up too. He suggested that we both sit down again. I agreed. I was lying. When he sat down, I remained standing. It turned out that there was something inexplicably unnatural and disorienting about trying to proselytize a custodian while he is standing over you. We came to a non-verbal agreement that neither of us was willing to surrender the high ground, and then I sat down.

For his next trick a Bible magically appeared in his left hand. I was impressed. I remember thinking, "I bet this guy could pull that book out of my ear like a quarter in a magic show."

He tried to get me into a discussion on specific verses in the New Testament. I immediately thought back to my ninth grade civics class. The teacher, Mr. Cerano, was constantly trying to provoke me into debating him on current events. I always wanted to, but I never did. I knew from experience that I couldn't come out on top in a debate with him no matter how good my argument was, because he was a civics teacher and a virtual encyclopedia of current events and I was a fourteen-year-old pothead.

Mr. Cerano never taught me jack about civics, but he did teach me a very important lesson about debating: if the playing field is not level, you lose at the exact moment that you agree to participate.

I refused to get into a discussion with Reverend James about the contents of the Bible. I like to win. He, like my civics teacher before him, was quite fond of the type of psychological warfare where the traditional concepts of winning and losing are convoluted and do not apply.

Winning for these guys has nothing to do with the content of the discussion that you have with them. If it did, it would be possible to imagine a scenario where at the end of a spirited dialogue Reverend James would say, "You know, I never really thought about the Gospels that way, Don. I think I may have been wrong all this time. Thank you so much for giving me this new way to think about it. As a result of your thoughtful analysis I am going to go home now and reevaluate what I have done with my life."

I guess anything is possible in this world, but I'd be willing to bet a year's salary that if you ever heard those words from the lips of Reverend James, they would be marinated in sarcasm.

Because his battle is being fought for the attention of the class, the civics teacher becomes victorious as soon as he gets the kid with the attitude problem to participate in the debate.

Because the Reverend's goal is to create a dialogue in the hope that it will lead you to join the congregation and drop some percentage of your income into the offering plate each week, his battle is also won at the time that you agree to participate.

The battle you think you are fighting during the discussion is irrelevant. By that point the war is already over.

I thought to myself, "He can pull that book out of my ear, saw it in half and put it back together, turn it into a rabbit or a bouquet of flowers, but I ain't playin'."

His final maneuver was a sort of stage trick, something you might see in a play. He began in a very soft voice to talk about the wonders of a life with Jesus. As he moved into a recitation of the specific miracles that his personal relationship with the Lord had made manifest in his own life, his voice began a slow and steady increase in volume. Soon he was possessed with the spirit. His eyes were closed. His voice reached a loud crescendo of praise and then dramatically dropped down to almost a whisper.

It was at this point that I realized that the Lord had blessed this preacher with an impressive flair for drama and a tremendous gift for theatrical dynamics.

He began his final sentence in a nearly imperceptible whisper and ended it by bellowing the name JESUS at the top of his lungs while simultaneously slamming the magic Bible with his right hand.

It sounded like a gunshot.

It physically jolted me.

Unfortunately for him, it didn't jolt me into salvation. It jolted me into laughter. I had heard the term "Bible thumper" before, but I had never really thought about it. I had just witnessed someone actually thump a Bible.

It was hilarious.

Reverend Gary

Reverend Gary from the Waldoboro Methodist Church best represents the other type of religious official that I encountered at the nursing home. He was young, under thirty, a bit awkward and naive but an absolutely lovely man.

He would stop in on weekdays just to visit with the residents. He was always bringing them little gifts. "I was walking by a little shop in Damariscotta and I saw this shawl in the window and thought of you, Millie. You can wear it in the morning when it gets cold in here."

He was the kind of man who makes it impossible for cynics like me to paint all clergymen with my "Reverend James the asshole" brush. He was always doing things for the right reasons. He was gentle, kind, and incurably sincere. He seemed to be deeply honored just to be of service in the world. I never spoke to him but he had a way about him that made me curious about his church.

The Lord had heaped a great bounty of righteousness into the heart of this man. But for reasons known only to the Lord, He had chosen to withhold from the good reverend any and all oratory skills.

Reverend Gary was an agonizingly boring speaker.

It is rumored that one of his particularly uninspired sermons was solely responsible for the great Waldoboro narcolepsy epidemic of 1975.

The Sunday church service at the nursing home was a thing to behold. There were probably ten residents who actually wanted to be there. Life on his delegated Sunday with us would have been much easier for Reverend Gary if this reasonably coherent group were the only ones permitted to attend.

That was not the case.

For the staff, the Sunday service was the one oppor-tunity each week to get almost all of the residents out of their rooms so they could change all the beds at one time. This meant that everyone who wasn't strapped down got stuffed into a wheelchair and rolled into the function room for some mandatory Jesus.

Talk about a tough crowd.

All the sounds, smells and sights that I described earlier in this piece were difficult enough to deal with when they were spread out in fifty separate rooms. To experience them all consolidated in one space and to think about the challenge that stood before this poor inept orator was like watching a plane fall out of the sky.

I was leaning on my mop and watching the geriatric cast of a Fellini movie being wheeled in one by one and assembled before Reverend Gary. As he fumbled with his notes, my mind called up an incident in my life from a month earlier—my first paid performance as a musician.

It was a going-back-to-college keg party. Some students had hired a popular local rock band to perform and I was offered fifty dollars to open the show. When I went on it was still light and the kegs had just been tapped. The stage was set up on the back deck of the house and the audience filled the yard.

I played my little original songs for about forty-five minutes. I was completely ignored by the hundred or so college students in attendance, but the eight friends of mine who had turned out to support me applauded enthusiastically. I came through relatively unscathed, so I was very happy and optimistic about my future as a folksinger.

The band played loud rock music for the next hour and then took a break. It was dark. Kegs had been consumed. The audience that had previously been kind enough to ignore me was now intoxicated.

My friends persuaded me to play during the intermission. I did and a very unpleasant memory was created.

Somewhere in the middle of my second song the audience started to heckle me with, you know, some of the classics. "You suck! Get the fuck off the stage! Boo!" I just wanted to finish the song and leave, but before I could the soundman turned the radio on in the speakers that I was singing through. It is a moment in time that is frozen in my memory. In the middle of a verse my microphone went dead and out of the speakers came the voice of a disc jockey. "W B L M! THE STATION THAT ALWAYS ROCKS!"

I stood there for a moment with everyone laughing and booing and then just turned around and walked back into the house.

For the next six months the sight of my guitar leaning against the wall in my living room would give me chest pain.

There are millions of people who write songs and play guitar in America and only a few thousand who can make a living at it. These numbers reflect the magnitude of the forces that one is up against. I am writing this twenty-four years after my traumatic first paid performance. Reflecting upon it today, I have no idea how or why I persevered in the business. I suspect that my inherent stupidity has probably played a role. I think I performed for ten years and didn't make ten cents. I was, in the vernacular of my father, "numb from the ass up," so it just never occurred to me that all the available evidence strongly suggested a career change.

Today I am a firm believer in the theory that success comes to those too stupid to know when to quit.

Many musicians and music business professionals have told me that I suck. They're right. I do suck. I just came from a recording session today where the engineer ran my vocal through this thing called a pitch adjuster. And there on a computer screen a big red line appeared whenever I was sharp or flat. It was proof positive that I suck.

It is a true miscarriage of justice that, in the light of this irrefutable evidence, I have a career (albeit minuscule) while so many of my perfect-pitch, guitar-wizard associates do not.

The road to success in this business is strewn with the corpses of the dreams of talented musicians. It is a dead dream gauntlet that we walk. If a good voice and instrumental proficiency were all it took to be a success in this business, there would be a famous artist on every street in America. Berklee College of Music is churning out great players and singers by the hundreds every semester. In my opinion success requires one thing—a stubborn streak that can defy reason for decades.

This is exactly what I saw in Reverend Gary. He was an inspiration. What I had experienced at the keg party was a minor aggravation compared to the impossible situation assembled before him. My singing ability was Pavarotti's compared to his speaking skills. I was only trying to get away with singing original songs to a bunch of drunken teenagers. He was attempting to preach the gospel of Jesus Christ to the aged cast of *One Flew Over the Cuckoo's Nest.*

There was something true and pure at the core of this man that always managed to get him through his sermons in this theatre of the absurd with a dignity that defied the realities of the situation. I watched him on several occasions read from the Bible and then interpret a specific passage so that it might more readily apply to life in a nursing home. All the while a drooling old man in a wheelchair would be rolling his eyes back into his head and saying "babababababababababaaaaah." Above the sound of that constant percussive drone would be sporadic yelps, eeeks, groans, and other non-verbal, description-defying utterances.

Often, Mr. Simmons would interrupt the sermon to ask if anyone would like to see his born-again weener.

The good Reverend always seemed unfazed by the extremely surreal soundtrack that the residents composed for his service. He just did the right thing. He put the word out there with compassion and sincerity and didn't concern himself with the madness of the situation or the odds against his words finding their way into a coherent mind.

Occasionally an imaginary rat would climb up Mary's ass and someone from the staff would have to wheel her and her soul-piercing screech out of the service. Or perhaps the reverend would use it as an opportunity to cut short the sermon. But on most occasions he held strong to the righteousness at his core and delivered the sermon to the best of his ability.

One Sunday, after a relatively uneventful service by nursing home standards, I was leaning against the nurse's station waiting for the staff to escort the residents back to their rooms so I could sweep up. All the ambulatory residents were gone and about ten others were waiting in their wheelchairs.

Suddenly the halls of the building began to fill with the sounds of ragtime piano.

Soon, bewildered residents and staff members were converging around the old upright piano at the back of the function room.

While no one was watching, Mary had wheeled herself over and decided to put on a concert. We all stood in a semicircle and watched in amazement as this woman, who had lived in this building without uttering a coherent word for eight years, regaled us with a series of blues, rags, and silent movie themes.

We later learned that in her day Mary had been the piano player at a silent movie house. Back then a sheet music score would accompany each movie. This score would be performed live in the theatre while the film was being shown. In 1979 Mary couldn't say hello, goodbye, yes or no, but somehow the part of her mind where the music resided was fully intact.

No one at the nursing home had any idea what caused her to decide to perform for us that day. I suspect that any psychiatrist who reads this account has probably heard of many occurrences like it and could readily deliver a technical term and an explanation.

That may be true, but it's bound to be boring. So in the interest of keeping myself amused and trying to maintain some shred of continuity in this meandering story, I am going to make up an explanation.

I can do that you know. I do it all the time—no biggie. I just step into my seven-year-old mind, rub my hands together and say, "Wouldn't it be cool if . . . !" And then I make up the coolest thing I can think of.

Here goes.

"Okay, okay, listen, listen. Wouldn't it be cool if there really was a God—no, no, wait, listen, this'll be great. So there really was a God and when he looked down from like, heaven or whatever, and saw the righteous Reverend pluggin' away every week—you know, trying his best to preach to this group of old fogies, who don't even know where they are. So like, when God saw how hard the guy was tryin' he rewarded him by letting one of his boring sermons kick open a door in some old lady's head where all this really awesome music had been hiding for like fifty years. That would be the coolest, wouldn't it?"

Mattie

Of all the residents that I met during my time at this job, my favorite was Mattie Campbell. She was a poet, a humorist, a brilliant storyteller, a philosopher, and a dear friend. I adored her.

Mattie was from another century. Her stories were enchanting. They were from a time of horse-drawn buckboards. It was a time when survival in winter depended upon two things: moose meat and reliable neighbors.

I was twenty-two years old. I had no marketable skills, no car, an infant son, and a job that paid me twenty dollars less a week than what I needed to pay my bills. I was able to whine with impunity about the inherent unfairness of my situation to anyone I knew—anyone except Mattie.

One day I made the mistake of complaining about having to hitchhike to work down Route 220 all the way from Stickney's Corner in the freezing cold. She sat in her wheelchair and gave me the annoying but irresistibly charming maternal grin of a woman who had lived the early part of her life in one of the most inhospitable economic and geographic places in America. Hers was a time when the likelihood of actually seeing an automobile with your own eyes and the likelihood of bumping into the Queen of England at the general store were about the same.

I stopped complaining.

A nurse had just left her room one day after making sure that she took a half a dozen different pills for her myriad of ailments. Mattie then handed me a notebook opened to a specific page. "What's this?" I asked. "Why it's my epitaph," she replied.

> *Here lies Mattie.*
> *She had a million ills.*
> *It wasn't those that killed her.*
> *It was the half a million pills.*

One time I told her about a problem I was having. I was in desperate need of money. I needed to borrow four hundred dollars from my parents. The problem wasn't whether they would loan me the money. I knew they would. The problem was internal. I didn't want to admit to them that I couldn't make it on my own, that I still needed my parents.

She was lying in bed. I was sitting on a chair that I had pulled up next to her. She said to me, "It's your responsibility to let people help you." I had no idea what she was talking about. She then asked me, "How do you feel when someone that you love asks you for help and you are able to help them?" I said, "I love that feeling, Mattie." She said, "So, the feeling you get when you are able to help someone that you love is a feeling that gives you great happiness, right?" "Yes Mattie, of course it is." "Then why would you insist upon making sure that the people who love you never get to have this wonderful feeling?"

It was one of those moments when a simple thought changed the way that I saw the world.

She had just induced in me a significant emotional growth spurt and while synapses in my brain were recalibrating to accommodate this evolutionary reconfiguration, she quietly dozed off to sleep.

*****

Nursing homes are Saint Peter's waiting room. Like a conventional waiting room, it may take a while before you get to see the doctor—a decade in some cases.

Eventually the nurse comes out and calls your name. "Mr. Wichenbach, the doctor will see you now." The doctor puts your life on the table, takes its pulse, looks in its ears and down its throat, and then hands you a diagnosis: a life wasted or a life well lived.

Unfortunately for many nursing home residents, the criteria for a life lived well when viewed by a person who is a month from the cemetery may hold little or no resemblance to the criteria that person employed throughout life.

During my time as a staff member in Saint Pete's Waldoboro waiting room, the saddest thing I saw was not the forced bathing, the Alzheimer's patients, or the stinky old men. It was the look in the eyes of the people who had lived insular lives.

John Bishop was eighty-nine years old. He had worked forty-five years in a mill. He had not been a bad guy—certainly not evil or anything. He went to his job. He went home. He watched TV. He yelled at his wife. He blinked his eyes and clicked the heels of his work boots one day and the next thing he knew he was lying in a nursing home bed, staring at the ceiling and trying to make sense of his eighty-nine years.

I hated having to go into his room to empty the trash. It was the saddest place I had ever been. A lot of the rooms reeked of urine. His room reeked of despair. The magnitude of the hopelessness that hung above him was overwhelming.

Mr. Bishop spent his last years scanning his life with the searchlight of reflection. Sadly, all the things that had brought him comfort in his earlier years—the promotion to foreman, the brand new '64 Chevy Bel Air, the pension— brought him no peace whatsoever in his last years. The rules had changed and he had found out too late. He and the others like him at the home would have given anything to be able to climb out of that bed and go back and live their life with more heart. They each longed desperately for one thing and one thing only—to be like Mattie.

Mattie's life made sense. It was a great source of comfort and peace to her. It was a delicate work of art. It was a ballet. Nearly ninety years of triumph over adversity with grace, dignity and, above all, kindness. She was born of kindness. She built a life of kindness. She melded it gently with compassion and wisdom and it rained down from her and nurtured every living thing in her world. If selflessness is what gives value to a person's life, then Mattie was the wealthiest person I have ever known.

I spent time with her every day. The sun always seemed to be shining in her room. As she approached the end of her life I came to believe that the light wasn't shining on her, it was coming from her. I learned many things from our conversations. However, the most valuable thing she taught me did not come from anything that she said. It came from the fact that I was the one person in the world who got to be with her each day as she approached the end of her life.

Her greatest gift to me was allowing me to witness up close the glorious final months of a life well lived.

It is unfortunate that so many people, as they approach the end of their life, seem to think they have no further opportunities to contribute something of value to the world. They spend their last months bemoaning their lack of contribution in their pre-nursing home years and ignoring the fact that fate, in its wisdom, has placed them in the easiest place in the world to maximize the impact of one's contribution.

Where does a kind word, a cup of tea, or the ability to listen have more value than in a nursing home? It has always seemed like the end of an Alfred Hitchcock movie to me when I see someone like Mr. Bishop keep himself in misery because he can't dive backwards into his life and show some kindness—while in fact he is literally surrounded with opportunities to do just that.

There was no such problem for Mattie. With every waking moment she threw white light effortlessly around all the dark places in that building.

In the last month of her life she continued to share great pearls of wisdom with me even though she was confined to bed and failing. I would tell her about my problems and challenges. She would listen with her eyes closed. Sometimes she would open one eye and say something like "Are you sure you're being honest with yourself?" Then, before I could mount a feeble defense, her eye would close and she would annoy and bless me with her knowing smile.

Mattie stayed alive until the last moment that she was

able to be of use to someone. When her health failed to the point where she was in too much pain to do so, she gathered up her beautiful memories, stopped eating, and checked out.

I missed her terribly.

A few weeks after her death I had a dream.

I put absolutely no value at all on dreams. All but a fraction of the dreams I have ever had are completely ridiculous and incomprehensible. So much so that if any of them were made into a movie, that movie would probably win an award at the Sundance film festival. However, everyone on earth who wasn't a performance artist or a film student would know immediately that it wasn't provocative or challenging, but just stupid.

Here's a typical Don White dream. I'm in the kitchen with my mother—not my today mother, my 1974 mother. She asks me to get her a can of soup from the shelf in the basement stairway. When I open the door to the basement, I am in California—not a basement in California, a roadside. I'm hitchhiking with a girl I went to elementary school with. We see a river. We dive in and when I come up out of the water I am in the reservoir off of Parkland Avenue in Lynn, Massachusetts. The girl is gone. Several of my friends from high school are partying on the shore. I swim over to them and ask if any of them dove into a river in California earlier today and emerged here. They have no idea what I am talking about and then I wake up.

I am not mystified, challenged or even mildly intrigued by this dream. I know exactly what it means. Nothing. Great big irrelevant piles of pure, unadulterated nothing.

It's as if the cat sat on the remote control and my mind changed channels every three seconds until I woke up.

I believe that when I go to sleep young art students overpower the security guard at my gate of reason, take over the studio and make movies. Being a creative group, they push the boundaries of conventional filmmaking by experimenting with things that have never been tried before.

"What if we create a really scary scene—something graphic and ghastly but we have him see it all very matter-of-factly as if it were a casual daily occurrence?" "Great idea Jeremy. And then tomorrow night we can do the opposite. We'll create a normal everyday scene and we'll give him the feelings of terror that he should have had the night before. Then we can study him as he wakes up in a cold sweat and tries to figure out what important message is being sent to him by his deeply troubled subconscious."

My subconscious may occasionally be troubled, but he never uses dreams or metaphors to communicate with me. We have been together a long time and he knows one important fact about me. I am very lazy. So if he ever tried to communicate with me via some elaborate, metaphor-laden dream, I would either take it literally or ignore it completely and in either case fail to get the message.

When I need to be told something from way down, wherever the hell it is that he resides, he always chooses to be blunt instead of clever. It will sound like this. "Hey, genius. You're acting like an ass. Stop it. It's stupid and it's pissing me off." The Don White subconscious is less of a subtle Buddhist master and more of a construction site crew chief.

I have, however, had some very entertaining dreams. My favorite one is entitled "The Flying Hockey Stick."

In this classic thought-provoking piece of science fiction I am standing on the corner of Waterhill and Cottage Streets near my parents' house. I have my hockey stick with me and I am trying to cross the street. I am being prevented from doing so by an unrelenting stream of traffic. I turn the hockey stick around so the blade is facing me. I stand on the blade and it becomes a flying stick. When I pull the handle toward me I go up. It also moves me left or right and lowers me when I push it away from my body. I fly high over the traffic.

I soon begin to think that this must be a dream. Immediately the stick starts to lose power and instead of being able to fly above the treetops I can just barely get up over the cars on the street. I realize that the magic flying hockey stick loses power whenever I doubt that it is real. My ability to use it to acquire and maintain the freedom of unrestricted flight is proportional to my willingness to embrace blind faith.

Deep, huh?

Anyway, so after Mattie died I had this dream. Well, that's not really true. I'm making this part up. I'm trying to hold this story together and I'm thinking that a dream revelation sequence will help.

In this fake dream, I walk into Mattie's room. She and Reverend Gary are sitting together on a couch. They each have their right hands closed and facing up. I walk over to them and they open their hands. In their palms they each hold a thousand tiny shining jewels.

The more self there is in a person's behavior, the farther that behavior is from the sublime. Conversely, there is a piece of eternity in each selfless moment. When you make the decision to use a moment of your life to do something kind or compassionate without wanting anything in return, that moment gets compressed into a diamond. If your life hands you a bunch of these jewels at the end, you win.

I Forgive You

I only want one thing in this life—to be the guy with the most jewels at the end.

There is no more formidable opposition to the acquiring of this goal than hatred. Hating someone is like carrying a big rock up a mountain. It serves no purpose other than causing you to exert additional energy with every step of the journey. If for some strange reason you actually have a practical need for a big rock when you get to the top of the mountain, there is an excellent chance that you'll find one up there.

The man who pressed a pistol against my son's head and took his wallet victimized everyone in my family twice. The first victimization consisted of robbery and terror. The second and infinitely more diabolical one involved the planting of hatred in the garden of our life. We all lost some youth that day.

We addressed the issues of the initial crime against us by putting the wagons in a circle, drawing the nucleus of the family in close and replenishing the reservoir of our love for each other. Everyone was left on their own to deal with the second one.

I had no control over the first crime. I was forced to deal with the short and long-term ramifications of it. The second crime is something altogether different. I was not forced to provide fertile soil to these seeds of hatred. Participation in the nurturing of this weed is voluntary.

Remember Mr. Blakeley—the guy with the green car? Well, one of the particularly annoying facts about the anger that I harbored for him is that it had virtually no effect on him. I never saw the guy. We avoided each other. So when the sight of a green car removed me from a sunny day on Tower Hill and hurled me into an imaginary lambasting, which one of us had been yanked out of a beautiful day? Which of us was incapable of enjoying that moment of his life or contributing something positive to the world around him? Certainly not Mr. Blakeley. He was on the other side of town and presumably having a wonderful time. His day was still sunny.

Let's take this up a thousand notches to the mugging. If the anger that resulted from what was essentially an arrogant snub at my wedding could infect an afternoon two years later simply because I saw a green car, at what future time would my intense homicidal *hatred* of the man who mugged my son allow me one single moment of peace?

The answer is never.

What could I possibly see, hear, or think about in the course of a day that wouldn't remind me about how good it would feel to kill this guy? My world is full of triggers for my hatred. When I sit in my living room I see my son's middle school graduation picture, his sister, his mother, his guitar. When I turn on the TV I see a cop show or a commercial with a young person in it. Maintaining this degree of hatred essentially poisons every aspect of my existence.

This hatred certainly does feel good and it is perfectly justifiable. There is even a strange sort of comfort after a while in the familiarity of it. In fact, it always seems like the right way to feel except when you look at it from the finish line.

I want to win.

This man stole, at gunpoint, a significant portion of

my family's youth and innocence. Why in the world would I also voluntarily hand over to him my ability to create a life well lived?

Fuck him.

That's right, fuck you.

I forgive you.

The Dinner Meeting

OK, everyone sit down. Before we eat I have a few important matters that need to be addressed. The first thing I want to do is to congratulate all of you on the tremendous job you have done. What this small, dedicated group has accomplished has been nothing short of astonishing. It's been a heck of a run, hasn't it? I mean, when we first took on this project everyone said we were crazy. But look at where we are now. We have fulfilled and exceeded every single goal that we set for ourselves. I am extremely proud of each and every person at this table. It has been a great honor and a privilege to work with you.

Having said that, I must regretfully announce that this will be our last night together. Tomorrow I will be betrayed by one of you and shortly thereafter I will be put to death. No, I am not going to tell you which one of you it will be. Suffice it to say that as time marches forward he will be the one disciple that no one will ever name a son after.

I'm not going to lie to you. I never lie. It hasn't always been easy working with you guys. I know it's been hard for you to process a lot of these new ideas. But I must admit that I sometimes felt that the entire three years was a series of situations where I articulate an idea beautifully and poetically and then we get together after the sermon and you guys are all, "What the hell were you talking about out there? Why should the meek inherit anything? Did you really say that if someone steals my coat, I should give him my shirt too? This shirt cost me five dollars."

I'll be honest with you. There were lots of times when I felt like a man forced to teach advanced calculus to a class of special ed students. Never mind what advanced calculus and special ed are. That's not important. What I am saying is that it could be very frustrating at times but I made the decision early on that I wouldn't let it get to me. And that I would always take the time to sit you down and say "OK, I'll explain it so even you guys can understand it."

I did that because I know how difficult a lot of this has been for you and to your credit you all worked very hard to get the message. You're a great bunch of guys and I really appreciate your commitment and everything that you have done for me.

I have done my very best to get all this new information out to the world. Now that the job is essentially over I am trying not to think too much about how it will be misquoted, misinterpreted, and manipulated by future generations. I keep telling myself that my job was just to get it out there and that I really can't concern myself about what will become of it in the future.

However, there is one thing I really want you guys to try and get right. I am going to talk about it now and I want everyone to take notes and try to reassure me that you will not screw this up.

During my crucifixion I will look toward heaven and I will say, "Forgive them Lord, they know not what they do." Has everyone written that down? Do I need to say it again? Simon, "know" is spelled with a "k."

OK, when I say that from the cross, what I am really saying is, "Forgive the people who are killing you."

No John, I did *not* mean to say, "Kill the people who are forgiving you." I meant exactly what I said.

Listen to me. This is important. I am not going to be here to answer your questions and straighten out your problems forever. You are going to have to learn to do this for yourselves. Forgiveness is a tool that I am giving you to unburden your heart from anger and sadness so you can be free to build lives of compassion and joy. That's what I want for you. I want you to be compassionate and joyful. And you'll all be relieved to know that forgiveness is something you do not have to be a genius or a high priest to understand or to utilize. This is for everyone.

Let me dumb this down for you.

Your heart is my home. I will live there with you and it will be a place of joy. When you are mistreated, hurt, betrayed or angered and you carry hatred in your heart, that hatred pushes me out of my home. I will stand outside the door and wait for you to forgive the one who has harmed you. Your forgiveness will evict the hatred from your heart and I will move back in. This is not mystical, magical or beyond the comprehension of the simplest among you.

I know how much you all loved the walking on water and the fish and bread episodes. I've got to be honest here. I just did that stuff to hold your attention. This forgiveness thing is *not* like that. It's a very simple, practical tool that everyone can use toward the goal of maintaining a light heart and a wonderful life.

Try to remember this. When you forgive someone it

doesn't mean that you like what they did to you. It doesn't mean that you want them to do it to you again. It doesn't even mean that you won't poke them in the eye if they do try it again. What it means—the only thing it means—is that you refuse to carry the weight of hatred in your heart, my house.

You have no idea how much I love you. You are all a great joy to me. Take this gift and use it. Please make sure that it gets written down the way that I explained it here today so that all my children can also use it to take care of themselves.

That's it. Let's eat.

Judas my friend,

please pass the lamb.

Afterword and Acknowledgments

Three weeks prior to my son's college graduation I took him out to lunch at the Blue Moon restaurant. He was at a point in his life where the world to which he had grown accustomed was sweeping him to the curb. And although he was intrigued by the whispers of the unknown softly encouraging him to take his first steps into adulthood, he was, as one might expect, more than a little unnerved by the uncertainty of it all. I thought that it would be a good time for us to spend an hour or so in an atmosphere that was conducive to serious conversation.

Had we lived at that time in Cambridge I would have brought him to one of the coffee houses favored by the local literati like Café Paradiso in Harvard Square—a place where so many profound ideas have been exchanged, pondered, and debated over the years that the air inside smells like overheated gray matter.

To a person unaccustomed to looking beneath the surface, the Blue Moon would seem an unlikely second choice for this conversation. But to me this is the one place in our community that has always been staffed and patronized by the deepest thinkers of our time—all brilliantly disguised, of course.

Take, for example, the existentialist poet masquerading as a burly bartender with an attitude problem. Or the forty-year-old neoplatonist working incognito as a waitress whose use of the phrase "youse boys" always gives an additional layer of cover to her true identity. And let us not forget the Zen master in the corner booth cleverly concealed beneath the persona of an unkempt middle-aged man who eats keno for breakfast, scratch tickets for lunch, and football scores for dinner.

Over two orders of chicken parmigiana we talked at length about several important decisions that were patiently awaiting my son's safe passage into the land of mortgages, salaries, and inadequate medical coverage. Eventually, the conversation turned, as these conversations often do, to relationships.

Toward the end of our meal I took a paper napkin and I wrote these words on it: "One excellent decision." I held it up for him to read and then I folded it in half and then in half once more. I handed it to him and said, "Put this in your wallet. You only get one of these. Use it when you are deciding who to marry."

After an awkward pause, I continued. "If you use your one excellent decision on anything other than choosing who to build a life with, it doesn't really matter how well thought out your subsequent decisions are because they all have to pass through your crappy marriage. It's like changing your oil but not your oil filter.

"Son, it can be argued that your father has only made one good decision in his entire life. In fact, now that I think about it, if you are looking for a decision-making rule of thumb, you might try asking yourself what your father would do and then do the exact opposite. The one obvious exception to this argument is that I married the best person I ever met.

"Your mother is, far and away, the best person I ever met. It was true when I was sixteen, and I have not met a single person since who could convince me that it isn't just as true today. No one else comes close. It's her heart. That thing is enormous. There is room enough in there for all the unfortunates of the world. Her compassion is not philosophical—she doesn't analyze a situation and then come to the logical conclusion that empathy is the proper thing for her to feel. She *is* empathy.

"And son, empathy is a hard thing to fall out of love with.

"If you are fortunate enough to marry a woman who embodies compassion, her compassion will influence every decision that you make in your life. It will force you to at least consider suppressing your warrior genes and take into account the other party's perspective. Of course, it's your responsibility to strike a balance here because an undefended heart is extremely easy to take advantage of and the world you are about to step into is laced with those who are anxious to do just that. But as you stand guard at her open heart and defend it from vandals and vampires it will slowly pull you inside and force you to see the world from empathy's perspective.

"And ten years later you'll be a girl.

"I'm only half kidding about this. Remember when your mother had her emergency surgery and we were standing beside her bed while the nurses were prepping her? Well, after you left and before they wheeled her out, she started to cry. She asked me to wipe her eyes because she was hooked up to an I.V. and couldn't do it herself. I took a tissue and carefully wiped her right eye and then her left. While the nurse was rolling her down the hall, I folded the tissue and put it in my pocket. Why? Because if something terrible happened and she didn't make it out of surgery, I would have treasured those two teardrops until the day I died.

"How girlie is that?

"Just about as girlie as it gets, son.

"Twenty years ago there was only one degree of separation between me and the keno Zen master over there. Eighty percent of my life was biker bars and football pools.

"Now I treasure teardrops.

"I hope you live a long time. I hope you live to be a hundred years old. If you are lucky enough to have a long life you're probably going to spend your last few years looking back at what you did with it. And son, trust me on this, you're going to want to see a million hugs and a million I-love-yous.

"Partnering in life with a big open heart accelerates a man's natural progression toward sentimentality. This room, this town, this world are all filled with men who, if they live long enough, will become comfortable, even anxious to shower their family and friends with the kind of undefended emotional expressions of love and caring that they thought would threaten their alpha male status when they were younger. And that's good—you know, better late than never. My advice to you is to climb inside a big heart and get those I-love-yous going as early as possible.

"And by the way, 'sentimental' is only a negative word when it hits the wind from the lips of a primate. If I ever get around to writing that book that I've been threatening to write for all these years, it will be sopping with sentimentality. Because, on a personal level, I can't help it, all these years with your mother have just made me that way.

And, on a business level, I have a theory that half of the money in the world is spent *by* women and that the other half is spent *on* them. So, unless you're selling jock straps or hockey pucks it's probably not a bad idea to give some thought to how women see the world.

"Look, I have no idea what makes a relationship work. There are probably as many answers to that question as there are people in relationships. Each person brings ten tons of luggage with them when they get involved romantically with someone else. Then they mash it together with the ten tons that the other person is carrying and just hope for the best.

"The people you think are perfect together don't last a year and the people you don't think will last a year stay together forever. As far as I know, Melinda and Damian are still what I guess you could call 'happily married' even after she threw his stereo onto the sidewalk from their second floor porch and ran him over with their car. Relationships are absolutely unfigureoutable. The people in them don't even know why it is working or why it is not working.

"I can point to several things that I think have helped your mother and I build and sustain a good marriage. We both come from the same town. We are both pretty good under pressure. And, of course, laughter—I would venture to guess that there are very few people who have been married as long as we have that make each other laugh as often as we do. I'd like to think that for the most part, deep, warm laughter has been the recurring theme and soundtrack of our life together.

"These are all important parts of our relationship but I do not believe that they would have flowered so beautifully had they not been planted in the deep rich soil of compassion.

"I think it's important to try to find someone that you

have a lot in common with, who can handle pressure, and with whom you can share laughter. However, I caution you not to use your one excellent decision on a potential marriage partner with any or all of these qualities but to instead unfold it and place it gently at the feet of the woman with the biggest heart."

"Thanks Dad. I really appreciate that. But I've got to be honest with you. You're embarrassing the hell out of me. Now stop crying and pay the bill."

*****

First and foremost, I thank my wife Theresa for letting me view the world for all these years from my home inside a heart so big and beautiful.

Thanks to Mark McInerney for bringing his tremendous creative talents to the cover art.

Thanks to Matt Watroba for pretending to be the publisher and writing the jacket copy.

Thanks to Steve Rapson for his invaluable help in researching the printing world and locating the best deal during a very challenging time for my family.

There were several people early on in this process who took the time to look at early drafts of some of these stories and who were all extremely generous with their time and in sharing their knowledge about writing with me as I approached this endeavor with an abundance of enthusiasm and a dearth of knowledge. I am very grateful to them all: Suzanne Brockman, Roz Cummins, Ed Gaffney, Michael Hill, Ralph Tufo, and Linda Weltner.

The more I learned about the traditional relationship between writers and editors, the less enthusiastic I became about entering into one. I kept clinging to this fantasy that somewhere there was a person who could edit in a way that would ensure that the text stood up to grammatical scrutiny while resisting the temptation to cleanse my personality from the stories. I was also delusional enough to think that an editor that I was paying should be willing to defend his edits to me. Then I could, in theory, learn the things I needed to know about writing but would have veto power over edits if I could successfully rebut the argument.

When I shared my fantasy with people who had any experience with editors, they just patted me on the head and said, "I think it is so adorable that you still believe in such things." Every time I walked away from one of these conversations I would wonder if I had just explained my thoughts on what an editor should be or if I had unknowingly just told that person that I believed in the Easter Bunny.

Then Steve Rapson suggested that I contact Terence Hegarty. I did. And that is why there is a book of my writings today.

Terence Hegarty. What a gentle soul he is. Rather than resenting the fact that I expected him to educate me, he seemed to relish the opportunity. (Not always perhaps, but for the most part.) I expect I will never meet anyone who loves language more than this man. An interesting turn of phrase seems to make him high. He will read it or listen to it, become distant for a minute, and then return to the conversation with what appears to be an afterglow.

Brilliant, patient, passionate, and sensitive to a fault, he soon became more concerned about what he called "my voice" and how it should be preserved at all costs in the editing process than even I was. He took it upon himself to attend a few of my concert performances to make note of how I spoke—the inflections, the nuances, the colloquialisms. He then took all of that into consideration while editing these stories.

I am grateful to him beyond words. And I am proud to call him my friend.

www.DonWhite.net